Mothering in Greece
From Collectivism to Individualism

BEHAVIOURAL DEVELOPMENT:
A SERIES OF MONOGRAPHS

Series Editor
RUDOLPH SCHAFFER
University of Strathclyde
Glasgow, Scotland

Furnishing the Mind: A Comparative Study of Cognitive Development in Central
Australian Aborigines
G.N. SEAGRIM and R.J. LENDON

Acquiring Language in a Conversational Context
C.J. HOWE

The Child's Construction of Language
W. DEUTSCH

Pre-School to School
N. RICHMAN, J. STEVENSON and P.J. GRAHAM

Theory and Practice of Observing Behaviour
G. FASSNACHT

Mothering in Greece: From Collectivism to Individualism
M. DOUMANIS

BEHAVIOURAL DEVELOPMENT:
A SERIES OF MONOGRAPHS

Series Editor: RUDOLPH SCHAFFER

Mothering in Greece
From Collectivism to Individualism

MARIELLA DOUMANIS

1983

ACADEMIC PRESS

A Subsidiary of Harcourt Brace Jovanovich Publishers

London   New York
Paris   San Diego   San Francisco
São Paulo   Sydney   Tokyo   Toronto

ACADEMIC PRESS INC. (LONDON) LTD
24/28 Oval Road
London NW1

United States Edition published by
ACADEMIC PRESS INC.
111 Fifth Avenue
New York, New York 10003

British Library Cataloguing in Publication Data

Doumanis, Mariella
  Mothering in Greece.—(Behavioural development)
  1. Mothers—Greece
  I. Title   II. Series
  306.8'743'09495   HQ759

  ISBN 0-12-221360-2
  LCCCN 82-82940

Photoset by Paston Press, Norwich
Printed and bound by T.J. Press, Padstow

Preface

From 1968 until 1977 I visited Athenian and rural Greek homes, in the context of three different research projects, in order to observe the mother–infant interaction in its natural setting.

I now realize that during this time most of my academic lectures, seminars, counselling sessions and exchanges with friends and colleagues were tinted with narrations of personal experiences and insights gained in the course of these observations. Quite often these impressionistic narrations evoked a vivid interest in my listeners, who inquired about further reading on the subject. Yet I did not dare recommend the scientific publications where the results of the research had appeared, because I knew that they would find there little if any of the information that kindled their interest in the first place.

I had always accepted that the most meaningful part of a research project of this kind is necessarily left out of the written presentation, until several colleagues pressed me to think otherwise. I am particularly indebted to Rudolph Schaffer who encouraged me to write this book, which draws heavily on my personal impressions.

In the course of this book I have tried to reconstruct the social climate in which the mother–child interaction takes place in two different settings, a modern metropolis and a rural village. I have tried to examine mothering as part of a way of life and not as a reflection of intrapsychic forces at work. The comparisons made throughout this book between the traditional and the modern only serve to highlight the influence which modern living exerts on this most central of human relations. In essence this book is about modern society and its ability or inability to raise children who can look at the past with tenderness and to the future with hope.

My intimate contact with other women's daily lives made me realize that we need to move away from our own constricted reality and into other people's worlds before we can realistically weigh up and eventually cope with our conflicts and contradictions, our strengths and weaknesses; both our own and those of the society we live in. This sense of perspective, which I gained by submerging myself into a traditional culture and sharing other women's daily life, is what I wish to communicate through this book. I hope that it might be of value to others as it was to me, as a woman, a mother and a social scientist.

Mariella Doumanis
Athens 1982

Contents

TO ALEXIA AND MARINA

Introduction

This is a book about Greek women and children who are now at the threshold of the technological era, bearers of a pre-industrial agrarian tradition, trying to come to grips with modernization and progress; it is about social change and its repercussions in the daily lives of young mothers and children, their attitudes, hopes and aspirations. It is a book written by a Greek woman trying to put together 15 years of personal experience and scientific research.

As a first generation Athenian (with both parents born in villages), raised in material comfort and offered choices and options of action undreamed of by past generations, I entered adulthood in unbridled optimism; in the front guard of a generation believing that in a world that offers so much, so much more than ever before, happiness was there for all the competent men and women to take and savour for life. With affluence replacing want, freedom substituting social coercion and no price to be paid for the deal. A distant echo of traditional values, direct contact with the progressive thinking of Anglo-Saxon Academia, the theoretical equipment of a social scientist, the experience of a practicing psychologist and the personal experiences of a working mother, comprised the treasury from which I drew the reserves I needed to pursue my quest for personal development.

Now, midway through life's journey (statistically speaking), the time has come I feel for me to pause and take stock*; to draw together personal experiences, professional observations, second-hand information and data from personal research and to assess the art of being a woman, beginning with its oldest and most stable of manifestations: motherhood. During my early adult years I considered mothering a simple and natural task, adequately performed by the vast majority of women, to the satisfaction of

---

* 'Here is Edward Bear, coming downstairs now, bump, bump, bump, on the back of his head, behind Christopher Robin. It is, as far as he knows, the only way of coming downstairs, but sometimes he feels that there really is another way, if only he could stop bumping for a moment and think of it . . .' (A. A. Milne, *Winnie-the-Pooh*).

both mother and child, reserving an attitude of pity and blame for those few exceptions who failed to live up to their role requirements. Children's problems and difficulties were exclusively, I believed, the result of maternal mishandling, and as such, valid criteria for maternal inadequacy. The 'proper mother' concept was at the time rather nebulous, encompassing such global concepts as loving care, psychological stability, and peace of mind.

During the late fifties, this attitude represented the way of thinking of both laymen and experts alike. It was not until the mid-sixties that developmental psychologists began focusing on the variables and behaviour patterns constituting maternal care. With the proliferation of observational studies of mother–child and especially mother–infant interaction, the image of the 'adequate' mother started to acquire a clearer contour and precision of detail; she emerged as sensitive and perceptive to the child's state, responsive to his needs and actions, gently and firmly rebuffing his inappropriate demands. The implicit prerequisite to such behaviour was her immunity to most of the turmoils of modern life, her wise appraisal of the challenges and opportunities it offers and her wholehearted devotion of all (or a large part of) her time and energy to the care and company of her offspring.

Studies of institutionalized infants demonstrated the developmental lag of infants lacking just this appropriate responsiveness to their actions, needs and demands. Language development experts saw mothers imitating their children's speech, expanding on it, using short baby talk sentences barely more complex than the ones used by their two-year-old children and in short, submerging themselves into the child's reality. Statistics indicated that, no matter how much a mother talked to her child, only if her talking was directly related to the child's actions and vocalizations would it be conducive to increased vocalization on the part of the child.

The clearer the picture of the 'proper mother' emerged from psychology manuals, the sharper the contrast between the textbook image and the behaviour of the mothers I befriended, counselled, taught and briefly encountered, in the streets, playgrounds, shops and restaurants, in town and on holidays; and the sharper the contrast between my own behaviour and the 'desirable' one. The image of the calm and contented adult at peace with herself and the world, who could care and give unconditionally, was in my eyes closer to fiction than to reality. The difference lay not so much in the specifics but in the overall climate in which the transactions took place: i.e., the curiously perfunctory care mothers lavish on their children (as very well described by Lasch, 1979) as opposed to the concerned attention and effortless responsiveness called for by psychology manuals.

For ten years I taught and counselled, giving advice and 'direction' to mothers and future mothers, leading them in the 'desired' direction. At the same time, I sought self-knowledge and awareness exposing myself to criticism and confrontation, 'searching my soul and airing my feelings.' The implicit assumption behind all this activity was that child-rearing is in itself a natural task tailored to the potential of every healthy (physically and mentally) woman and the inability to perform this task adequately is a sure sign of inadequacy, warranting intervention. This inadequacy was viewed as either deriving from a mere lack of information, due to the secluded way of life of the urban woman and her minimal contact if any with small children prior to the time she becomes a mother, or it was attributed to immaturity, faulty behaviour patterns and extreme intrapsychic conflict, warranting more in-depth psychological treatment. As experience began to accumulate, however, at both the receiving and administering end of the counselling profession and as clinical practice sharpened my perceptiveness and observational skills, the subtle and not so subtle information I was acquiring began to shake some of my basic assumptions. I saw active, intelligent and creative women overwhelmed by the task of child care. I saw committed mothers and housewives irritable and empty-hearted at the end of many a 'comfortable' day at home with the children. I saw colleagues and laywomen alike perplexed, embarrassed and even guilty *vis-à-vis* their children and I began to wonder, if we were to label all of them 'inadequate' mothers, who were the adequate ones?

Are we defining mothering in over-idealized terms? Can the rather pronounced amount of lassitude, irritation, indifference and anger we sense and occasionally see in mothers around us be simply part of 'normal' mothering? Has it always been so at other times and in other places, including the traditional rural Greek milieu where the image of the Mother with a capital 'M' was born and nurtured for several centuries? Are we in our time faced with patterns of social organization which tend to undermine and weaken all stable human relations, the mother–child relationship included?

The feeling of dissatisfaction with the quality of personal relations appears to be so pervasive in most developed countries, and so many people in rapidly developing countries like Greece are relating progress to precariousness in human relations, that it becomes hard to dismiss the problem as non-existent; denying the social aspect of the difficulties in human relationships and just focusing on each case that comes to our attention, treating it as a deviation from the 'norm'. If social variables are at the root of much of our presently-felt malaise about personal relations, the acquisition of specific techniques of communication coupled or not with intrapsychic reshuffling could hardly be an effective remedy for the problems at hand, particularly if we ignore the causative factors.

The question, as it presents itself now, is not whether or not our way of life does indeed create difficulties in the sphere of human relations, for this seems to be a widely acknowledged fact. It is the specific nature of these difficulties and most importantly the possibilities left for stable and meaning-ful human transactions within the existing social frame that need to be investigated further. In a time of acute economic crisis we define as healthy and successful the business which goes through the fiscal year with minimal losses. Are the present-day social conditions such that they call for a redefinition of mothering along the same lines? It may very well be that in our day and age the role of the mother in its optimal condition is one of limited returns, aspiring to the avoidance of profound crises and disillusion-ments. Maybe the 'adequate' mother is the one who barely pulls through the task of child-rearing, large doses of irritations, disappointments, boredom and anger included, provided she does get some occasional satisfactions and her offspring grow up thinking of the relationship as one that was not all bad after all. Should this be the case, it is admittedly a far cry from the romantic notion of the mother–child relationship I held twenty years ago.

It is an image I find hard to accept as optimal for any social group and especially for the one that holds such a central and cherished position in our society (like in most). In modern day parlance, if all mothering has in stock is minimal daily satisfactions and a vague existential appeasement, given the large investment of energy, responsibility, care and money the role requires, it may very well soon turn out to be a non-profitable 'business' threatened with extinction. Unless, and this is a very pessimistic hypothesis indeed, it survives because the returns in many other areas of investment of human creativity are becoming meagre as well.

As I observed the mother–child transactions and listened to Athenian mothers talk about their daily lives, time and again I came up with a general feeling that something was missing in the relationship. 'Something had happened' sometime, somewhere, that was depriving the relationship of its stability and direction, and that 'something', whatever it was, was poorly understood and seldom acknowledged. It was as if mothers were ashamed to admit that they were having a hard time performing their role. Somehow, there seemed to be a gap between the rhetoric of the 'importance of motherhood' and the role in action. Between the profoundly sad longing of the childless woman and the irresolute attitude of so many mothers *vis-à-vis* the child care tasks, there seemed to be a discrepancy hard to understand. I wondered why for many women the awareness that they cannot have a child becomes so shattering an experience while, at the same time, for many mothers child care is a task that leaves them almost empty-hearted and as a result with feelings of guilt. The rhetoric was I thought greatly coloured by past reality, molding the attitudes and inflating the expectations of future mothers, while the daily task of child rearing was very much shaped by present-day conditions, which somehow seemed to interfere with the satis-faction obtained.

Motivated by the desire to seek an answer to these questions and especially curious to compare present-day patterns of mother–child interaction with traditional ones, I embarked 8 years ago on an observational study of mothers and children in a rural milieu where progress had not yet taken its toll. I conducted, at the same time, similar systematic observations among working class Athenian families of rural origin.

Greece in the mid-seventies still offered a good opportunity for social scientists to have first-hand contact with people living in communities functioning on the basis of pre-industrial patterns of social organization. At the same time, many people of rural origin lived in the periphery of a large cosmopolitan capital, leading a way of life typical in many respects of an industrialized (not yet fully technological) society. In other words, Greece offered an opportunity to study simultaneously two points (landmarks) along the social evolution continuum, leading from a simple rural way of life to a complex modern one. This I did for two years, 1975–1977, in the hope of discovering what is happening to the role of the mother in Greece, as a result of economic progress and technological development.

In the chapters that follow, I shall attempt to retrace my steps in the discovery of the traditional Greek family and its urban working class counterpart. I begin in both cases with a brief resumé of the social dynamics of the place and gradually focus on the family constellation and the mother–child interaction in particular, where the most emphasis is placed.

Although most of the information I now have on this domain was obtained in the course of doing a structured research project, the presentation I shall attempt here is a personal one, devoid of statistics, graphs and tables and based primarily on the subjective impression I formed from my contact with the urban and rural people whose daily lives I shared and observed. In my wish to do justice to all the fine nuances I sensed and observed in the families I visited, I chose to stay away from the presentation of quantitative results focusing instead on all the meaningful details which are excluded from a scientific presentation and can only fit within a personal narration.

1   Purposes and Procedures

The basic reason that led me to look for the answers to some of the poignant questions about motherhood in our time, through the study of a traditional model, is probably directly related to the fact that I am Greek. For centuries the mother figure occupied a central position in the Greek milieu, clothed with a mystical aura which made her the object of deep respect bordering on veneration.* It seems certain that the discrepancy I was experiencing between the role expectations and the role performance of motherhood was to some extent due to the values I had inherited about the mother role; values which were somehow out of time and place in late twentieth century Athens.

As I set out to explore the mother–child interaction in the traditional rural Greek milieu, I was intrigued to observe closely the behavioural patterns that sustained such an idealized image, and I was eager to discover patterns of daily behaviour that bore the distilled experience of centuries. I believed at the time (and still do today) that, in a setting where a long line of generations have lived under quite similar conditions, the stability and continuity of the life sequence gives rise to patterns of social organization that can stand the test of time. Through repeated exposure to similar situations and problems people are bound to arrive, through successive approximations, at ways of meeting life's demands that are compatible with human needs in a synthetic global way. On the other hand, the very young complex technological culture which we live in today offers fragmented solutions to the satisfaction of human needs, presenting the individual with continuous conflicts of interest. By attending to one area of human activity, social, family, professional, civic, etc., we necessarily neglect the other to some extent.

---

* In a survey of a representative sample of Athenians, conducted in 1960 (Vassiliou), 29% of the respondents gave in a sentence completion test for the concept of 'Mother' highly idealized responses, like, a madonna, a goddess, the golden blanket covering us, etc.

Having experienced my full share of role conflict throughout many of my adult years, I was very curious to experience, even for a brief period of time, the taste of a life free of such conflicts and contradictions. I knew from the beginning that the specific solutions that emerged in a simple rural community would not be transferable to our complex and fragmented world, but I was hoping, by submerging myself into the order and harmony of an old cohesive culture, to unlock a door to universal meanings. Being a social scientist as well as a questioning mother, I was looking for new experiences as well as research data that would help me decipher my experiences. Thus this investigation into motherhood took the form of a controlled research project designed to meet, as closely as possible, the requirements of research methodology.*

In the pages of this book I attempt to map the life of the young mother in two different worlds, our complex modern one and the simple, traditional, rural one. The main emphasis is placed on the influence social factors exert on the daily mother–child interaction and the historical, social and economic forces that mould it. In order to delineate the social field of which the mothers are a part, I had to move far outside the limits of my own discipline assimilating and incorporating within this study facts and information from other fields of study. My aim was to begin by mapping the traditional rural Greek milieu, defining in general terms the principal dimensions of social organization and the historical conditions that bore and nurtured them. As a second step I intended to examine the mother–child interaction, looking for the repercussions of the social structure on the daily routine of the mother–child pair.

The ideal way to conduct such a study would be through the close and extended collaboration of a historian, an anthropologist and a developmental psychologist, whereby each one would study the two specific areas (the rural and the urban) from his own viewpoint and the results would be presented synthetically as an integral whole. Setting up such a research team was, however, well beyond the possibilities of an independent and self-financed researcher. As the next best solution, I chose to rely on the historical and anthropological information already available, which is presented in chapters two and six. The historical and social information is selectively abbreviated and presented as a background for the analysis and understanding of the observational data on the mother–child interaction.

This approach is based on the assumption that the anthropological accounts of various rural Greek communities bear direct relevance to the

---

* The results of this project were submitted in 1978 as a thesis for the degree of Ph.D. at the University of Lancaster.

specific villages where the interactional observations are conducted. Evidence in support of this assumption may be drawn from the anthropological studies, for reading through them one realizes that from Campbell's Sarakatsan village to Friedl's Vassilika and DuBoulay's Eubea village, to mention but a few, basic similarities may be noted pertaining to the patterns of social organization which may be considered typical of the traditional, rural Greek community despite marked differences in local mores and customs. The presentation of the common elements from within the anthropological studies, which in my opinion characterize the traditional rural Greek milieu, was based on my own frame of reference and may be of little interest to ethnologists and anthropologists to whom this presentation is bound to appear too broad and general. The historical–social introduction addresses itself to the non-specialized reader and is only designed to serve as a background for the understanding of the social dimension of the mother–child interaction.

With this word of apology to fellow scientists from other disciplines for trespassing within their own domains, I shall now focus on my personal contribution. The rural setting I chose to conduct my observations in was a semi-mountainous region of Epirus, a north-eastern part of Greece where tourism and industrialization had not yet markedly interfered with traditional village life. From five neighbouring villages (Rahi, Kostakioi, Kalamia, Halkiades and Gramenitsa) twenty mother–child pairs were selected for observation. A young psychology graduate, Angeliki Stamati, acting as my research assistant and myself spent about three days in each of ten households. Part of the time was spent in systematic observation of the mother–child interaction while a considerable part of the visits was spent interviewing the mother, chatting with the people present and socializing when the situation called for it.

Adhering to the basic principal of research methodology which dictates the need for a control group, another twenty mother–infant pairs, from the low income zones of Athens, were selected for systematic observation. The experiences and the data collected from the two groups are compared and contrasted. In the pages that follow, I shall not present what has already appeared as a doctoral dissertation, I take this opportunity instead to record the personal impressions, thoughts and ideas born from this experience, that usually remain untold in a dissertation, and also to present other people's findings as they stand out in the light of my own experiences.

A. The observation

Psychologists have been well aware for the last 20 years that by asking mothers to report on their child-rearing practices they obtain one version of reality and by observing mothers in action quite another. Of the two versions, the most objective one is likely to be the second and, although a much more difficult one to record, it is the one that is most commonly accepted by developmental psychologists as a valid source of information. Psychologists wishing to observe mother–child interaction must by necessity spend much longer hours collecting their data than would be needed if they were just asking questions. They also have a much more cumbersome process of data analysis to face.

Despite the considerable amount of effort the observational method necessitates, the returns can only be said to be more valid and detailed than those obtained by other more indirect methods. Observational data can hardly claim any absolute objectivity. In the case of naturalistic observation in particular, the presence of the observer within the observational field causes an interference which is hard to measure and even harder to overcome. As my personal experience has taught me, the particular influence the observer exerts on his subjects differs from one setting to the next and from one individual observer to the other, no matter how much effort is being made to standardize the observational conditions. For example, my assistant and I found to our surprise that our presence was more of an interference in the Athenian households than in the village ones, despite the fact that we were culturally closer to the Athenian than to the peasant mothers. Athenian mothers were used to performing their mothering and household tasks in almost total privacy, a situation which we disrupted by our presence. In contrast, rural women lived and worked in the midst of a continuous flux of relatives and neighbours of all ages coming in and out of the house at regular intervals throughout the day. Used to performing under the continuous scrutiny of in-laws and neighbours, they were hardly perturbed at all by the presence of an unknown observer whose value judgement was of little consequence to them. Once the initial surprise was overcome, and the mothers realized after the first visit that all we were going to be doing was sitting, observing and taking notes,* we felt somewhat assimilated within the frame of the household. In the urban families on the other hand our presence was always adding an unusual dimension to the mothers' daily routine.

The second surprise that our field work had in store for us, illustrating the highly variable nature of the observational situation, was related to our implicit assumption about our interaction with the mothers and their behaviour towards us. Although we were unaware of these assumptions, the whole project was based on the expectation that mothers would behave towards us in the way we professed to behave towards them, i.e. pretending

---

* The observational instrument used was the one devised by Clarke-Stewart (1973).

to ignore us and to focus on the child instead. As is common practice in studies of mother–child interaction, we told our subjects about our interest in the behaviour of the child, avoiding to mention our interest in the mother for fear of intimidating her. Thus, while we planned in each case to violate the norms of proper social conduct and watch carefully although discretely all maternal behaviour, we assumed that our subjects (the adult ones that is) would go about their daily business as instructed, acting as if we were not there.

In the first rural household we visited we were in for quite a surprise. From the moment we entered the house until we left, the mother's undivided attention was on us. This was true for the household I visited and the one visited by the second observer, as we later found out when we compared our impressions. During the first half hour of the first observation we were both flabbergasted, for we were unprepared for what we had experienced. When I say I had the mother's undivided attention I mean that she just sat opposite me motionless and stared straight into my face without asking questions or volunteering information for what appeared to me a very long period of time. During this period I just observed the child interrupting every now and then to talk to the mother. Gradually, and as I was recovering from the surprise, I realized that her behaviour expressed a very straight wordless set of questions: 'who are you?'; 'what are you doing?'; 'what do you want from me?' and I can still recall that, despite my strong concern about the possibility of carrying on the project as planned under the circumstances, I did not feel uncomfortable or ill at ease. After all, I was there to find out about her as much as the tools of my trade allowed me to and she simply did the same. So, every now and then, I volunteered some small piece of information about myself, my professional context and my project and she responded with some information too. I was more than grateful during that time for all the anthropologists had taught me through their studies about the milieu I was observing. This knowledge gave me a 'déjà vu' experience, which I could not predict but I recognized it when I saw it. It made me realize quickly enough that the behaviour I was observing (which seemed so unusual to me) was not due to the mother's individual idiosyncracies but was an aspect of the behaviour pattern I was there to study.

As it turned out this first encounter was a kind of screening test for us. On the basis of their observation the mothers decided what kind of a relationship they were to establish with us, and so did everybody else in and around the family who came time and again to give us a good stare. After this first screening, all the mothers in the subsequent visits turned to their daily routine leaving us to our task, exchanging a few words and a few more stares with us and invariably inviting us to more intensive socializing after our observation time was over.

Well before we computed our data we knew that the rural mothers' observational skills were quite unusual by our standards. The first indication we received was the differential treatment bestowed on the two observers. Before I explain in detail what I mean, there is one point I need to clarify about our visits to the villages. The field study in the rural setting was not completed in one continuous stretch of time. For personal/family reasons, and in order to control for seasonal variation, we made several trips to Epirus interpolated with the collection of data in the Athenian setting; we thus left and returned to Epirus four times.

Starting for our first trip back to Athens, we noted that I had received several gifts (oranges, eggs, walnuts etc.) from the families that I had observed, while my young colleague had received none from the ones she had observed. We assumed that I must have just happened to come into contact with more generous people and did not give it a second thought. When exactly the same thing was observed on our second trip back we began discussing it in detail.From our discussions during the long drive back to Athens, we realized that our expectations of the observation were markedly different, and each one of us simply received the treatment she implicitly expected. I had embarked on this project with great eagerness to come into contact with the rural people, getting to know them as intimately as possible and learning from them as much as I could. I knew that any kind of personal relationship in this setting entailed a lot of give and take and I was quite pleased to receive presents from them, being ready to reciprocate with what they told me or I guessed they needed from Athens. I also trusted their wisdom and I felt certain they would only give me what they could spare, so I was very much in favour of this give and take. In contrast, Angeliki became involved in this project more out of interest for the job, her first one after graduation from college, than the village life and what she learned from her contact with the peasant mothers was a secondary gain that merely satisfied her intellectual curiosity. Fresh out of college, with most of life's questions still unanswered, the discovery of Athens was bound to be for her far more relevant than the peasant tradition. She was thus friendly and very amiable towards the mothers but not particularly eager I suppose to become over involved with them; and the mothers acted accordingly. Interestingly enough, after we had talked about this matter at some length and acknowledged our differential expectations as something inherently related to the different life phases we were in, on the last two trips back from Epirus Angeliki's share of the gifts began to increase. At first it comprised a few flowers from the garden and gradually became more substantial, including oranges and lemons.

Most mothers would give us 'something to take back to our family' on the last visit or when we dropped by to bid them farewell before leaving for

Athens. In some unforgettable instances, however, their gifts came as a high point in a very intense non-verbal communication. In one instance, which was clearer to me than most, I was interviewing an eighteen-year-old mother; she was sitting opposite me with a very small table in-between us, which I used to place the tape recorder and my note pad on. Her own mother was sitting next to me in total silence, the child had disappeared at the other end of the yard in some relative's house.* In the still of the summer morning, sitting comfortably under the thick shade of a grape vine quite close to one another, as I can now recall, some imperceptible bonds developed between us. Our individual differences ceased to count and we were just three women sharing our child-rearing experience simply and directly; one doing the asking, another answering and the third just listening, yet to all three many memories and feelings associated with mothering had come to the forefront of our awareness. If the experiences were different for each of us, the mood was common and bound us together at that moment. The questions I was asking were related to maternal expectations, fears and hopes about the future of the mother–child relationship, and the answers I was receiving were short, steady and clear. Involved as I was with the young mother and her answers, I heard some faint noise on my right side and I remembered the grandmother, whose presence I had momentarily forgotten. 'Blessed woman to have such a daughter' I thought to myself, astonished by the peacefulness and security that came through the young woman's answers. At that moment, the grandmother got up and disappeared into the house, to return a few minutes later with a paper bag full of eggs; she just placed them on my lap with the comment 'these are today's eggs from our own hens'. I felt very moved and I just smiled in gratitude, more for the experience than the eggs. This silent acceptance of my presence, of all of me as I stood there stripped of credentials, connections, past failures and achievements, whenever it came, manifested with a token, a gentle hug on the arm or a timely smile, gave me a feeling of deep satisfaction and comfort. On such days in the Epirus villages, I could work for twelve hours in a row without a trace of fatigue.

The ambiance in the Athenian household I observed was in many ways different. I felt grateful to the mothers for accepting me in their homes and embarrassed for intruding into the privacy of their family life, intrigued by what I was observing, admiring in some cases, critical in others, bored occasionally, but my rapport with the urban mothers was in no case as intimate as with the peasant women. My social role as an expert was at all

---

* This household was not included in the final sample, for the living conditions prevalent (the husband being in the army and the mother living with her own parents) were rather exceptional by traditional village standards.

times as important in the relationship as my physical presence. In the emptiness of the urban flat I could feel my presence acquiring undue importance as the mothers were striving to make a good impression. Many of the mothers focused their efforts exclusively on the child, as if their assumption was that the more they did for and with him the better. Others tried to excel on all fronts, especially during the first visit, trying to meet all at once the requirements of the 'proper woman' as advertised by the mass media (mother, housewife, socialite, glamour girl, all in one).

In the urban households, Angeliki's presence must I believe have been much less of an interference than my own. A young unmarried girl could more easily establish a working relationship with the mothers on an equal basis, allowing them the security of their experience and keeping for herself the credit for some professional knowledge. In my case, the fact that I was older than the mothers and had personal and professional experience in the area made many of the mothers look up to me as an authority figure rather than a human being. Unfortunately, it was the urban mothers with whom I could identify most, whose experiences were more similar to mine, who assumed that the social distance between us was the greatest. Nothing as subtle and gentle as a look, a smile, or a meaningful silence could bridge the gap of suspicion and awe separating the layman from the expert. Only a verbal statement could possibly reveal the hidden similarities binding two human beings. But words tend to be loud and awkward allowing no smooth retreat if unwelcome and I dared not make such a statement, remaining instead a distant expert to the end of the visit in all Athenian households.

I did not dare reveal to any of the mothers how many times in the past I had myself felt awkward and embarrassed in the presence of someone I had assumed to be all knowledgeable. Nor did I dare say how misplaced I now consider this attitude of humble acceptance of expertise to be, as far as human affairs are concerned. It took me many years to realize that it is life's experiences, pain, despair, anger, hope and delight, fear and courage, and the willingness to experience them all to the fullest that gives human wisdom its substance. Professional knowledge, facts and figures only come as embellishments, adding texture, details and contrast to the inscribed form. If personal experiences are too shallow, professional knowledge (in the human domain) can only add up to a blurred undefinable whole, offering no direction or purpose.

B. The sample

Having decided that forty was the maximum number of mother–child pairs I could possibly handle, given the laborious process of data processing that my observational method entailed, I aimed at selecting two groups of mothers (20 urban and 20 rural). They had to differ as little as possible in all respects but the setting they lived in, as my intention was to focus on two groups of mother–child pairs representing the norm in their respective settings. On the basis of my previous knowledge about the milieux under study, I drew the demographic profile of the average rural and working class Athenian young couple and then proceeded to choose mothers in my sample to fit this profile as closely as possible.

All the mothers I chose were non-working, between 18 and 28 years of age, married for no more than five years prior to the birth of their first child and with a clear medical record. The rural mothers were married to farmers not older than 40 years of age. The urban mothers were married to blue collar workers again not older than 40 years of age earning a monthly income of 7–10 000 drachmas (which offered at the time a somewhat comparable income level with the rural families, not in terms of money but in terms of living standards). They all had first-born children 14-16 months old; the children were all delivered with a normal child-birth, weighing 2.5 kg at birth, with a clear medical record and no medication given to the mothers during labour. Half the rural and half the urban toddlers were boys and half girls. The urban families were selected from the files of a maternity hospital, the rural families from the files of an ambulatory well-baby clinic. The urban mothers were either natives or Athenian residents for a minimum of ten years; all came from families of rural migrants. I thus ended up with a selected and not a representative sample and my observations can only give indications applicable to two very limited segments of the Greek population, the young Athenian working class mothers and the more traditional peasant mothers and their young children.

The life of the peasant women living in the semi-mountainous villages of Epirus in the mid-seventies cannot be considered typical of the traditional rural women living in the 19th or early 20th centuries. It was, however, close enough to the traditional model to offer a striking contrast to the urban way of life and as such was relevant to the aim of this study. As anyone visiting the traditional Greek villages can observe (those which are not totally abandoned by their inhabitants or invaded by tourists), with the passing of time these villages appear to age, and age markedly, rather than develop and change. They appear to have lost most of their strength and vitality but they have preserved their overall stucture despite a few misfitting additions here and there. Some of the houses are in ruins, especially the outer ring of the settlements, some appear unlived in and barely holding together, others are kept in good condition without any obvious alterations and still others, especially the ones close to the central axis and the main square, have been thoroughly modernized, occasionally keeping only the scale of the neigh-bouring houses and in other cases violating even that. Yet, if the village is seen as a whole from a neighbouring hill not too far away, its basic structure, charm and beauty are still apparent. The entire settlement appears as an organic whole and not an agglomeration of houses; a whole which is not superimposed on the landscape but, despite the sharp colour contrast, becomes an integral part of it like a clump of trees or a rock formation. One is invaded by a sense of rhythm, order and harmony as one gradually discovers the careful repetition of forms and details and their synthesis into an endless variety of interrelated patterns. The ruins add a depressing tone and the new models an element of discontinuity yet, by selectively directing one's gaze to certain parts of the settlement, the observer can mentally reconstruct the image of the village as it was during the period of bloom. Similarly, by observing present-day social interaction between a selected group of village women one can reconstruct parts of the social fabric and with a certain amount of generalization and extrapolation relate the present with the past, on the human as well as on the architectural level. The overall impression I formed of the rural mothers I observed, judging from their behaviour towards their children, husbands, relatives and neighbours and towards me, their values and attitudes as revealed by their answers to the questionnaire I administered, was that their way of life did not differ markedly from the life described by anthropologists a couple of decades ago. In some ways, their life style still reflected the patterns of social organization prevalent at the time when the Greek villages were semi-autonomous self-sufficient communities.

Needless to say that, along with the traditional influences, village women were absorbing many of the vibrations coming from the large urban centres. Although they did not imitate openly (at least the most traditional ones I worked with) urban mannerisms, their assumption was that life in the city was much easier and better than it was in the villages. This conviction, if it did not openly transform their attitudes and behaviour, corroded their belief in their way of life in a subtle and pervasive way. As for the urban sample of mothers, I have no way of knowing just how representative it was of the entire population of young working class women. I can assume, however, that as a whole they represented one of the most problem-free segments and the one adhering more closely to the traditional stereotypes. Young, but not unduly so, healthy, newly married to a working class husband with a healthy child born fairly soon after their marriage, they appeared to be of the less innovative type and the ones less likely to meet with striking success or disappointment.

C. Gaining co-operation

The most important and in many ways the hardest undertaking in a naturalistic study of mother–child interaction is, I believe, to gain the

acceptance of the mothers for the observation and sustain their co-operation.
In the more traditional Greek villages there appears to be only one smooth way of achieving this: through the mediation of an important person, who holds a key position in the village community, enjoying the people's full acceptance. After many trials and errors, I selected the well-baby clinic in the city of Arta, with its ambulatory unit servicing the neighbouring villages, as the medium through which to reach the local households. It turned out to be a very fortunate choice, for the institution and especially its ambulatory unit that I worked with, was exceptional in many ways. In contrast to most Greek institutions, which are notorious for their inefficiency, sloppiness and ineffectiveness, this unit was remarkably well-organized, with an up-to-date follow-up system and a personnel that was knowledgeable and most co-operative. The visiting nurse, in particular, who introduced us to the mothers, had gained the mothers' acceptance and was viewed as the likeable and trusted representative of an institution offering services which were needed and appreciated (medical examination for mothers and future mothers, medical examinations for babies at regular intervals, vaccinations, etc.). Born and raised in the Epirus area, the nurse had studied in Athens and returned to Epirus to work; she had an intuitive knowledge of the people and their ways. When she introduced me to the first household I was quite surprised by her approach. Having worked with her for a couple of days, going through the files to select the households for observation, I knew her to be a very gentle person. I was thus taken aback by her introductory statement to the mothers, which seemed to me discourteously brief and terse: 'Mrs Doumanis is here with us; she will stay and observe the baby for three days.' She then inquired about the baby's development, talked to him a little and sat silently while I made arrangements with the mother for the first visit.

Her behaviour remained a puzzle to me until I began writing about my experiences and I viewed it in the light of the local people's values and norms of conduct. There was no doubt that the mothers were offered no choice about our visits but, to my surprise, in their behaviour there was no trace I could detect of doubt or hesitation about accepting us or any discomfort for having done so. As I later understood there was no reason in this particular setting for doubt or discomfort. One of the fundamental differences between my urban outlook and the reality of the rural people is our differential predisposition towards unknown people. To urban dwellers 'people' in general often mean the crowds to be avoided if possible; usually we only wish to become involved with certain people under certain circumstances. In contrast, to the Greek villagers strangers* traditionally represented poten-

---

* In modern Greek as well as in ancient Greek, the word 'stranger' (xenos) is synonymous with 'guest'.

tially valuable information, stimulation, new opportunities and support. They were as a rule sought after, but with caution at first in order to screen out the malevolent ones.

In our case, since we were there on behalf of the well-baby clinic, introduced by the visiting nurse, if we were refused access this would mean a thorough breach of confidence with the whole institution. It was the nurse's responsibility to screen the persons she introduced; should my presence prove to be detrimental to the baby or to anyone else in the house the blame would go to the nurse and the clinic. If the mothers refused to co-operate they would be challenging the nurse's judgement, since mistrust is the only reason for refusing to deal with a stranger and not receiving him at home. Under the circumstances any polite questions or explanations on the nurse's part would have been superfluous and even misleading. The brief statement 'Mrs Doumanis is here with us' implied that they knew me well and took full responsibility for introducing me. What the mothers were presented with was a fact and not a decision demanding any critical judgement in order to select the best course of action, for there was no alternative. As dictated by the ingroup principle 'a friend's friend is our friend as well'; a principle developed over the centuries by people who needed to broaden their circle of social affiliations in order to survive but needed to minimize error as well, as we shall see in more detail in the chapter that follows.

If the mothers' judgemental skills did not come into play during the visitors' initial acceptance, all their observational and critical abilities were mobilized thereafter to assess the type of relationship called for by the visitor's personality and the given circumstances; and this is when the intense observation began as mentioned earlier.

In the urban households the situation was much less clearcut, with a lot of variation in the way we were received by the various mothers. In order to win the mothers' co-operation I chose a simple procedure of presenting ourselves at the door and, with the maternity hospital as a reference, trying to gain acceptance into the households. This approach was dictated by my earlier experiences from a similar study of mother–infant interaction I had conducted in Athens in 1968. Athens, however, changed so dramatically during the seven years that elapsed between the first study and the second that I doubt whether this approach is still the best one under the present conditions. Nowadays, most households have a telephone which they did not have in 1968, people are more familiar with receiving formal letters and are much more suspicious of strangers. If I were to repeat the study, I would first write an introductory letter then call to set an appointment for the first visit; with the hope of minimizing refusals and sparing the investigators the unpleasantness of having doors slammed in their faces, something I must admit I was totally unprepared for. I was aware that Athens was developing at an alarming rate and in the process undergoing drastic social transformation; I had read about it and I had sensed it in many ways, but still when I came face to face with the new reality I was shocked.

My colleague and I contacted 64 households in Athens in order to secure the co-operation of the 20 needed. The first thing that surprised me was the large number (20) of mothers who could not be located, either because the address recorded at the maternity hospital files was not the correct one, or there was no reply during two consecutive visits or because they had moved to an unknown address. What was new for me in this situation was the neighbours' inability or unwillingness to provide any information about the people we were trying to contact. In 1968, I had followed the exact same procedure in order to locate 30 households and there wasn't one I couldn't trace. If there was no reply from the house I was calling at, more often than not someone would appear within a few minutes from a neighbouring house, either in response to the repeated bell ringing or because we were seen from their window, and volunteer some information. If the neighbour did not know where the mother I was looking for was, I would be referred to someone else who was closer to her and was bound to know. There was not one family who had moved and had not given her new address to at least one of her ex-neighbours. There was not one mother, I can remember, who was absent from her house without someone knowing where she was and when she would be back. In 1968, only one mother refused to participate in the project and she did this most politely. In 1975, several mothers refused to open the door, although they were at home as revealed by the noises inside, and eight refused more or less abruptly to co-operate, either by slamming the door as the investigator began talking or by waiting until we had finished and then uttering a curt refusal.

The mothers who did agree to co-operate lived in much more comfortable houses than the ones I had visited in 1968, but they appeared more secluded within the confines of their new flats. Some treated us as formal guests while others viewed our presence as yet another 'must' in their daily routine. Why a 'must' I don't quite know. What intrigues me most is why, among the urban women who did have the possibility of refusing to co-operate, some gave the impression, subtly and indirectly of course, of forcing themselves into the role of hostess which they themselves had agreed to play. The rural mothers, who were not initially presented with such a choice, did not seem to question this role ever. The reason for bringing this question up is that I believe that the mothers' behaviour *vis-à-vis* an unusual visitor reveals one of the fundamental differences between the traditional and the modern way of life.

To the rural people the basic directions in life were given, handed down by tradition as the best and therefore the only ones proven by experience to be profitable for the individual; and as such they were taken for granted. In this context no question of freedom of choice could have arisen and I don't believe people could have felt oppressed by it. With the saving of energy (mental and emotional), ensuing from simply and unquestioningly following the given direction, rural people could exert all their creativity in performing the given task in a thorough and unique way. In my case some of the rural mothers did exactly this by discovering subtle ways of giving this rather unusual relationship intensity and intimacy.

In contrast modern urban dwellers are presented with a vast array of choices for most of life's situations; they hesitate, they doubt, they question the alternatives, unsure about the returns. They are often presented with the choices but lack the criteria by which to judge the respective merits. Due to the novelty and unclarity of many of modern life's dilemmas, many choices are made at random under the pressure of time and remain open to question ever after. Thus much of the available human energy is spent on the choice itself, revising the alternatives again and again with every new piece of evidence, i.e. experience accumulated. Similarly, in the case of this project, the urban mothers were faced with a rather ambiguous situation; they were presented with an option of accepting of refusing to co-operate but without any clear notion as to what they would gain or lose in both cases. They intuitively made up their minds and for those who agreed their word of acceptance was, in effect, committing them to continue with the project. Yet with each visit and while I was in their house they were bound to be reconsidering, explicitly or implicitly, the soundness of their decision on the basis of the gains and losses obtained or anticipated. Focusing their attention on the original dilemma, trying to discover the possible indirect gains from this experience and moulding their behaviour accordingly, they necessarily paid only limited attention to me as a person, discovering in the process little of the human being in front of them beyond the stereotyped label of the expert. It is sad to realize that in this way they deprived themselves of the only available gain, that of a potentially pleasant, albeit brief, human encounter. It is sad because similar incidents occur again and again in our daily lives and more often than not the questioning is unavoidable.

PART I
THE RURAL MILIEU

2 Social Structure: the Family, the Ingroup, the Community

Reading through the anthropological studies describing the patterns of social organization observed in various Greek villages, mostly during the fifties and sixties, one becomes impressed with the complexity of the social system, its coherence and integration. In a perfectly complementary fashion, institutions, moral values and norms of conduct converge into a clearly articulated whole, which defines the life and development of each community and of the people comprising it.

The scarcity of natural resources coupled with the oppressing demands of the ruling lords have resulted in a steady state of hardship for the Greek peasants. Their survival would have been impossible without a way of life geared to minimizing waste and error and maximizing returns from human and natural resources alike; a minutely calculated mode of action encompassing each and every aspect of human activity. The relative historical continuity in this milieu* allowed and even dictated the development of patterns of social organization incorporating the lessons learned from the past while at the same time leaving room for adjustment to new conditions and circumstances. In the course of several centuries a social system was developed, common in its general structure to most Greek villages and unique in its details for each one, whose universality bears witness to its effectiveness under the given circumstances.

This social system was patterned on the basis of inherent human contradictions, strengths and weaknesses and the given environmental conditions. It was a system founded on the philosophy of the carrot and the stick as behaviour modifiers, each provided in ample quantities and, most importantly, carefully balanced amounts. It was a system aimed at securing the

---

* A brief historical introduction is presented in Appendix I.

maximum of group solidarity and at the same time triggering individual responsibility and autonomous undertaking, minimizing experimentation and error without stifling creativity and exploration, triggering individual expressiveness and assertiveness while controlling violence and destructiveness.

The village community, small and homogeneous as it was, did not comprise for the individual a uniform group of people. It was sharply divided into subgroups to which one was related with varying degrees of intimacy, ranging from total identification to outward hostility. These groups were for each and every person his immediate family, his extended family, his network of ingroup affiliations, his outgroup and the village community; groups increasing in size and decreasing in intimacy in a clearly defined hierarchy. Every person had his kinsmen, his affines and his enemies; in this context the indiscriminate Christian commandment 'love thy neighbour . . .' was inconceivable. Behaviour was rigidly defined on the basis of group affiliations, with a different behaviour pattern adopted *vis-à-vis* the family, the ingroup members and the outgroup.

Each individual's group affiliations were related to his age and status and were changeable in the course of his life, i.e. people constituting an individual's immediate family formed his extended family in adulthood and people who at one point were his outgroup could through marriage become his extended or immediate family. As group affiliations changed, so did behaviour. Additionally, the strength and size of each family's extended and ingroup affiliations and so the number of outgroup families, were neither stable nor given, but varied with the family's success and status in the community. The various groups to which each individual belonged—interconnected, complementary and opposed as they were—formed a dynamic social field around each person which supported, stimulated and controlled him.

A. The elementary and extended family *

The father–mother–children nucleus, the way we know it in the cities as an independent unit, was non-existent in the traditional rural Greek milieu. In the latter, it was more of a conceptual entity based on an emotional and psychological differentiation, rather than an autonomous system with clearly

---

* Much of the information on the traditional rural Greek family is drawn from J. Campbell's book 'Honour, Family and Patronage'; an outstanding study of institutions and moral values in a Greek mountain community, conducted in the mid-fifties.

defined boundaries existing within the network of interrelated interests and intimate personal relationships characterizing the extended family. The concept of the elementary family and the parent–child relationship in particular constituted the primary bond, taking precedence over all else. The family was 'in the popular mind an earthly reflection of the Heavenly Family of God the Father, the Mother of God and Christ . . . through reference to a divine model, a man or woman in family life participated in a reality that transcended individuality; the harsh and ceaseless struggle to survive, even simple and often repeated actions such as carrying water, milking sheep or baking bread came to possess a validity which was absolute and intrinsic' (Campbell, 1964). In this context the obligations of parents towards their children possessed an absolute and sacred quality and were viewed as the all powerful and only acceptable motives for individual striving and achievement. Through parenthood, man and woman partook in the natural and divine order rising above human lowliness and weakness.

When a girl married, she left her parental home to join the household of her husband. For some 5–8 years after their marriage the young couple did not set up their own household, they lived with the husband's parents, his unmarried siblings and the married brothers, their wives and children. During this stage the services of the man and the woman as a worker belonged to the whole group. The young wife did not only care for her own husband, but she had to be ready to take up any hard or unpleasant work that needed to be completed within the household. The husband continued to attend to the family obligations he shouldered prior to his marriage. Until the birth of their first child, the elementary family went through a latency period during which conjugal solidarity, although gradually developing, was subordinated to extended family solidarity. 'The extended family was a corporate group owning in common all significant property; and of this the leader, whether father or brother, was the trustee not the owner. Economically it struggled to become a self-sufficient unit with a division of labour organized about the service of its flocks and the cultivation of its land; . . . . The individual in his work and behaviour was entirely committed to his family and in principle all members were held to be responsible for the action of any other member' (Campbell, 1964).

When a man's children reached the age of 4–6 his obligations towards them took precedence over all other family obligations. He was then pressured to become the head of a household, moving out of the paternal household and separating from his brothers. The assumption of the status of head of household was in itself a matter of prestige, making a man the equal of all the other heads of household in the community. When the eldest son reached the state when he had to assume the role of head of household, the father abdicated his authority (whether he wanted to or not) and the eldest son took over the responsibility for the management of the family estate. When the younger brothers married and had children of their own, the family property was divided among the brothers. After the division, the family fields or flock usually continued to be managed jointly but the returns were distributed in proportion to ownership.* Each brother's dwelling, when moving out of the paternal house, was built by all the brothers together in the immediate vicinity of the parental home. In many cases, the progressive additions formed an interconnected whole with a common outdoor yard in which women and children appeared to be leading a collective life. Even recently, in some of the households I visited I could not tell by observing people's daily routine who lived where.

Co-operation between the members of the extended family was for the Greek peasant or shepherd essential to his survival; a married pair and their share of land and/or sheep did not form a viable economic and domestic unit. Self-sufficiency, which was the necessary prerequisite to survival and stability, could only be obtained through the division of labour among several households forming a corporate group. For this reason, the association between kinsmen in the traditional rural communities was not solely an economic one; the economic bonds relating family members were strengthened by social, psychological and existential ties as well. The solidarity of the corporate family was symbolized in the idea of blood (αἷμα); a man referred to his family members as 'my blood', and it follows that he who loses blood loses strength. Family loyalty, which was a fundamental value in this setting, was supported by norms of conduct offering ample rewards to the person adhering to this principle and harsh punishments to the one disrupting it. The family would support any of its members as much as possible through their needs and hardships and would provide, to the extent possible, each member with the means to a good start in life; daughters would receive a dowry upon their marriage and sons part of the family estate. The family would, at great expense, educate its ablest son and/or would support a son to emigrate; the brothers would cultivate his land and attend to his flock in his absence supporting his wife and children until his return.

The family identification of one member with another was absolute, demanding unconditional loyalty and allowing no flexibility for widely divergent interests. An infringement of socially acceptable norms of conduct reflected not only upon the reputation of the individual, but also upon the general prestige of the family. Serious misconduct of any one member was

---

* The dowry each bride brought with her in terms of land bought or sheep added to the flock stayed with her own elementary family after the division of the family estate contributing to unequal property among brothers.

perceived as treachery to the group; this member's very presence from then on became a denial of the qualities and attitudes on which the harmony of its internal relations depended. The objectionable element had, therefore, to be excised for this was the only way in which the family honour could be reinstated. In many villages in Epirus, Crete and Macedonia, in the Sarakat-san communities and among the Maniot families in the Peloponnese, a father had to kill his daughter if she betrayed her virginity, a husband his wife if she voluntarily committed adultery. A father or elder brother had to expel from the family house a son or a younger brother who acted disloyally to his siblings, depriving him in extreme cases of his share of the family wealth. The father or brother who accomplished this terrible work won a grudging respect in the general community.

To us today the absolute authority the head of household exerted over his kin in the traditional Greek community is inconceivable and so is the amount of responsibility the culture attributed to the family as a group and its leader in particular for the behaviour of each one of its members. No man could bear to carry this responsibility without the security of knowing that he was fulfilling a sublime role in which he had full acceptance and support from his family and his ingroup.

B. Distant relatives, neighbours and fellow countrymen: the ingroup–outgroup dichotomy

The family, effective as it was in securing its members' daily living, could not offer a guarantee against extreme mishaps. The resources available to the traditional rural Greek family were always very limited and its level of functioning so dangerously close to the minimum level as to necessitate outside support in cases of serious crises, like prolonged illness, damage of the crops, death of the flock, etc. Each family secured the necessary supportive system by establishing links of interdependence with as many families as possible within the community and even outside of it. Co-operation between families would usually begin with the exchange of small favours, extending gradually to economic, social and moral support in times of crisis. Once a co-operative relationship was established between two families, each considered the members of the other as part of their ingroup. Friendships between individuals based on simple attraction were almost non-existent, for the energy and care the individual would invest in this personal relationship he would deprive from his family where his foremost loyalty lay.

Any relationship between two men automatically extended to both families and all their close associates and would be contrived only if it was beneficial to both families. Therefore, each family would tend to associate with socially equal or, if possible, superior families, increasing in the process its power, influence and social prestige in the community. In this land of scarcity, the progress of one family was seen as curtailing the other families' chances for similar advancement, unless there was an established interdependence between them. Therefore, outside the corporate family, social relationships were either positive or negative, with no room for neutral gradation in between. Families were either co-operating with one another, closely and intimately, or were competing aggressively, cunningly and sometimes fiercely. Every new person a man had dealings of any importance with was viewed as a potential ingroup member. The ingroup relationship between two families was established gradually through successive approximations, i.e. repeated exchanges of gifts and minor favours, testing each other's readiness to reciprocate indicating a perception of communality of interests. Once this communality was sufficiently tested and established then the relationship graduated into one of trust and intimacy, sustained through a ritual of offerings and counter offerings and often sealed with a spiritual kinship bond, 'κουμπαριά', whereupon the one man would act as a wedding sponsor at the other man's wedding or his son's wedding, or he would become the godfather of one of his children.

Like all relationships in the traditional Greek milieu, the ingroup association was defined in terms of operational criteria and tended to be both stable and flexible. In this setting, where strong social and emotional bonds complemented economic interrelationships, feelings, care and concern were not offered indiscriminately out of a diffuse sense of philanthropy; they were carefully invested and were neither withdrawn over trivia nor were they indefinitely given out sustaining relationships that had ceased to be operational. In defining an operational relationship in the rural Greek milieu, it should be emphasized that despite the fact that survival motives dictated most of the Greek peasant's actions, they did not ever operate unilaterally. Due to the maturity of the culture, material concerns were indivisibly interlocked with concerns about honour (τιμή), bravery (παλληκαριά) and generosity (φιλότιμο), integrating economic, social and emotional investments into an indivisible whole and in the process enriching the life of nearly dejected peasants with excellence, pride and passion. Similarly, human relations outside the family circle (as well as within) were nurtured by the social and emotional as well as economic gains derived by all parties concerned and were terminated in the case of either member in the relationship proving inadequate in satisfying any one of these three important aspects of human exchange. For example, when the community was evaluating a man's conduct (which it did all the time), his own ingroup people had to defend his actions. Where a man had behaved in a manner clearly at variance with the values of the community, a kinsman or friend was forced to abandon him (breaking his bonds with him) and even to take some part in condemning his conduct. For, if he continued to support his cause, his own reputation and that of his family would suffer. This he had to do no matter how serious the emotional and economic cost.

Through the network of ingroup affiliations, the traditional family expanded its boundaries beyond the limits of its immediate geographic location; the 'κουμπάρος' (best man or godfather) in the city might facilitate dealings with the government and the state officials, find a job for the migrant son or offer shelter to the one studying in the city. Within the village the relationship of trust, mutual confidence and affectionate concern between ingroup families operated like a protective shield. Friends and kinsmen would pass information to one another about all happenings in the community, they would confer together about any major action anyone had to take, validating his judgement and suggesting possible courses of action. Although each man carried for himself the responsibility of his actions, he had at all times a readily available 'opinion survey', indicating to him the socially acceptable course of action both in terms of material returns and social repercussions, coming from people he trusted and respected.

The strong, effective solidarity between ingroup members had as a counterpart the hostility and opposition directed outwards to unrelated families. Co-operation and opposition were in a way complementary, each strengthening the other. Through competition with the outgroup friends and kinsmen found the day-to-day attestation of their co-operation and sharing with each other. This took the form of standing up for their own people in public, exhibiting their solidarity with them and their controlled hostility to the others, publicizing, praising and magnifying the achievements of their kin and friends and scrutinizing critically the others, sharing successes with friends and blaming foes for misfortunes. The values of prestige and honour so central in the traditional Greek culture rested on the attention and opinion of friends and enemies, on the concerned interest of kin and the grudging acceptance of competitors.

The opinion of the outgroup was a strong factor in shaping individual behaviour. The role of censor and retributive justice was indirectly assigned to the outgroup in cases of individual weakness or divergence from the normative behaviour, leaving the supportive role to the ingroup. Although only a very close kin would actively scold, reprimand, or take action against a misbehaving person (adult or child), he would do so only in order to protect him and his whole family from the meaness of the outgroup who were readily awaiting to take advantage of the first sign of weakness in their opponents. The continued hostility and cold war situation among unrelated families in the community kept people in a constant state of readiness and vigilance allowing them the opportunity to practice daily their skills of cunningness, fearlessness, calculated aggression and bravery in defending their own and grabbing what could be had; skills vitally necessary for the survival of people living for centuries under foreign rule, exposed to the whims and aggression of the local lords and their entourage, foreign armies and bandits.

C. The village community

Despite the strong opposition between the various family groups, the village community operated as a well integrated system. With a few exceptions—as in the case of the inhabitants of Mani, in the Peloponnese—antagonism between the various ingroups seldom reached open warfare. Through an unwritten common law and often through the intervention of high status persons, like the teacher, the priest or the doctor, the cohesiveness of the village was maintained and the tendency for deceit and theft between antagonistic families was usually kept within tolerable limits.

Vis-à-vis the outside world (the Ottoman or the Greek Government, the landlord or the enemy) the community functioned as a whole, acting as a mediator between the local reality and the outside demands or adversity. Floods or drought, taxation or state loans had for centuries been met at the community level through the joint effort of all the families. During moments of crisis, passions and hostilities between competing families were put aside, to be resumed in full after the crisis was over.

In addition to the co-operation brought about by external threat or crises, the local identity was sustained through social activities in which the whole village community participated (funerals, feasts, weddings and celebrations of the patron Saint). Even the form and organization of the built environment seemed to contribute and reflect the community's cohesive social structure.

In concluding this brief survey of the social structure of the traditional rural Greek milieu, I feel compelled to restate my surprise and admiration at the complexity and integration of the system and its effectiveness in equilibrating the opposing forces in human nature under the given environmental circumstances. It will be difficult for the uninformed reader to share my enthusiasm for the intricacy and effectiveness of the social system described, from the few pages in this book which necessarily give only a gross outline. Through the anthropological accounts one can find detailed exposés of the gradations and nuances in the relationships between and within families, in the normative behaviour of people as related to the degree of intimacy between them, the conditions for the cooling or break of co-operative bonds, the shifts from an outgroup to an ingroup relationship and vice versa. These features all testify to the complexity of the system, its specificity and at the same time its lack of rigidity. Within the very specific and unchange-able structural frame of family–ingroup–outgroup, each family in a given locality had a number of different relationships defined on the basis of its particular needs. A family could have its closest and most significant relationship with a genealogically close or with a distant kin or even an unrelated neighbouring family, as dictated by mutual interests. The choice, although guided by certain general principles, was open to individual variation. From one locality to another, the violence between outgroup families varied considerably and so did the intimacy between ingroup members, the attitude towards visitors and the links between inlaws. All these variations in detail within the same structural pattern bear witness to the general principle of 'freedom within a frame' which prevailed in the traditional Greek milieu giving it its vitality and continuity.

By omitting all details of social organization and their intricate intercon-nections, I fear I have sketched a rather simplistic and inflexible social model. Yet it still becomes apparent how much this 'simple' social system offered its members. A man or woman in this milieu lived closely surrounded by supporting kin and friends and competing neighbours, provided with a set of clear and incontestable values, specific modes of conduct for most of life's situations, a stable hierarchy of priorities eliminating most conflicts of choice and with alternatives of action limited, in most cases, within the realm of collective experience. The assimilation of nature's rhythm into their daily lives and their identification with the archetypal model of the Heavenly Family provided traditional men and women with a sense of partaking of the natural and divine order. The reference to a perfect model imposed on people demands of absolute virtue which were achieved and safeguarded through continuous and consistent group pressure entailing immediate rewards and sanctions. With unlimited support and acceptance from kin in moments of difficulty or weakness, continuous control from kin and com-petitors to protect him from eventual tresspasses, socially acceptable outlets for his aggressive impulses directed to the outgroup, specific models in his immediate environment setting realistic standards of excellence, the harsh-ness of life to stimulate his survival instincts, family needs to motivate him for achievement and a reference to a divine model to appease his existential anxiety, traditional man could be righteous, proud and at peace with himself and the world.

What puzzles me at this point is how we modern urban dwellers manage to cope with life, stripped as we are of permanent and unquestionable values and clear norms of conduct for the many different situations we find ourselves in. We are deprived of support and of preventive controls, we lack acceptable outlets for hostility and aggression, have no clear models for co-operation, love and care and we have no convincing answer to our existential problem. It is a mystery to me and a tribute to human nature that we do not have more aggression, social apathy and debilitating anxiety than we actually do have in modern cities, where each man must fend for himself alone.

3 Rural Women

A. Role, status and identity

In the traditional rural Greek setting, the roles of man and woman were completely different, but complementary. The house was the domain of the woman; her responsibility was to attend to the physical and emotional needs of her family. Her role was expressive and responsive and her function was connective, symbolizing the love that bound the family together. The place of the man was outside the house in the community, where he toiled to keep his wife and children fed, safeguarding their interests, protecting them from assaults and representing his family to the outside world.

In a relationship of absolute interdependence such as existed between man and woman in the context of the corporate family, it is pointless, I think, to speak of a superior or inferior role. Despite the very submissive attitude a woman adopted *vis-à-vis* her husband, as we shall illustrate later on, her contribution to the emotional and physical survival of the family was far too important to be rated as secondary. The overall presence of the rural women I worked with in the Epirus villages and especially that of the elderly grandmother, who dominated the scene in most households I visited, can hardly be associated with the image of the 'oppressed woman' we so often hear about. The directness and intensity of their gaze, the absence of any sign of nervousness as manifested by their limited yet appropriate comments and actions during our first encounter and, most importantly, the warmth which they bestowed on me as the relationship progressed, I find hard to attribute to oppressed people.

Seeing the ceaseless struggle of these women and experiencing the peacefulness and self-assuredness they radiated as they proceeded in their daily activities, I have redefined for myself the notion of oppression, relating it not to the amount of discipline or hard labour imposed on the individual but primarily to the feeling of importance and worth, or rather lack of it, he or she derives from the given situation. In these terms, traditional rural women were far from oppressed. The main disadvantage of the female predicament in this setting, however, pertained to the fact that any claim to worth or importance could only be attained through motherhood, a condition not always attainable by all women. Only after she had had children could the traditional woman perform her important role as organizer, mediator and guardian of the family's integrity and cohesiveness.

During the period of her life prior to her marriage, which the young woman spent in her parental home, she performed within the organizational frame set by her own mother. As mentioned by the majority of Epirus mothers I interviewed, the 'proper daughter' was just expected to be 'obedient', that is to accommodate herself to the pattern set by her mother. When she married, as a young bride she usually moved in with her husband's family and there again she had to make every effort to fit within the existing order, as set by her mother-in-law. The status of the bride was traditionally rather low, as vividly described by Campbell in the somewhat extreme case of the Sarakatsans. The only way she could make herself appreciated was through hard manual work.

During the early stages of her marriage, the new bride was subordinate to other adults in the extended family and, in general, any hard or unpleasant work would be delegated to her. The bride would take most of her orders from her mother-in-law but she was expected to carry out requests from any brother, sister or senior bride of the extended family. Yet, despite her subordinate status, she was accepted as a full member of the group. 'She is one of us' they would say, implying that membership carried with it the possibility of a growing comradeship and the right to protection against insult and injury from outsiders. The young husband would give the minimum of overt public attention to his wife, he might make some simple requests of her for food and drink or dry clothes, but he would not make conversation. For her part, the bride would never address her husband in front of other members of the family. Clearly, the intention was to deny the importance of the sexual relationship between husband and wife, by avoiding any display of affective interest in each other. Since all members of a family used to live and sleep together in a typical one-room house, if a brotherly relationship was to be established and maintained between the newcomer and her brothers-in-law, every sign of the young woman's sexuality had to be suppressed. To this aim, the occurrence and frequency of sexual intercourse between the newly married pair had to be concealed as much as possible. Undoubtedly, the beginning of marriage was for a woman something of an ordeal. It was recognized by all as such but was accepted as inevitable, and the feelings of loneliness and despair the young woman experienced in her new surroundings, although appreciated, were only afforded a brief indulgence. 'When you are married you are enslaved because God wills it so' (παντρεύτηκες, σκλαβώθηκες γιατί ὁ Θεός τό θέλει) the women are still heard chanting today; and when they rock their babies they warn them of what lies ahead, 'Let him dance, let him rejoice now that he is in his youth, for when he marries he will meet with hardship' (Νά χορέψει, νά χαρεῖ τώρα πού εἶναι νιὸ παιδὶ γιατὶ σαν θά παντρευτεῖ μὲς στά βάσανα θά μπεῖ).

What was said above about the status of the bride is not applicable today, even in the most remote and traditional of communities. Although all the mothers I observed in 1977 in Epirus lived with or right next to their in-laws, their relationship with their husbands, even from the beginning of their marriage, appeared to be more intimate than was traditionally acceptable. Still, when I met them about 2–3 years after their marriage there were few, if any, signs of femininity in their appearance. When compared with the unmarried girls in the family, not only did they look much older than the chronological difference would account for, but they also dressed and behaved differently. The clothes they wore were too dark and graceless for their age and they were seldom heard chatting, singing or laughing out loudly. Interestingly enough, the one mother in my sample who constituted an exception to this rule was in permanent conflict with all her in-laws who lived next door and her mother-in-law in particular, as she personally reported. Her house was the only one where nobody dropped in all the while I was there and her only social contact was with the lady owner of the local grocery store.

After the birth of her first child the status of the traditional woman changed considerably. For the bride in the Sarakatsan families this change was most pronounced. With the arrival of the child the attitude of the whole extended family would shift from tolerance to acceptance and affection for her as the mother of their tiny kinsman. The care of the baby would be her exclusive responsibility and the demands placed on her time for breast-feeding and other attention it required would alleviate the amount of heavy house work she had to perform. At this time the husband's behaviour towards his wife would also undergo fundamental changes. He would begin to talk to her more freely before other members of the family. And in his presence no member of the extended family except the parents-in-law would any longer order her about in peremptory fashion, let alone attempt to scold or discipline her.

In essence, motherhood constituted for the traditional Greek woman a point of transition from the state of a worthless 'object' to that of a respected person. The dramatic difference between the social status attributed to the mother figure and that attributed to the woman took an extreme form among the secluded Sarakatsan communities, the Maniot and Cretan families. The difference did exist, however, in almost every Greek community, and still does today to some extent. As late as 1966, the attitude survey conducted by Vassiliou (as mentioned in Chapter 1) on a representative sample of

Athenians yielded evidence for this striking difference in attitudes. In contrast to the idealized adjectives provided for the concept of mother, the adjectives Athenians associated with the concept of woman were overwhelmingly negative, i.e. cunning, deceitful, superficial, loose-tongued.

This difference is still so strongly embedded in the mind of rural women today that they cannot even conceive of a *raison d'être* outside motherhood. One of the mothers I observed during the project's preliminary phase lived in a semi-mountainous village just 35 miles outside Athens. She was married for eight years before she became pregnant. Fifteen months after the birth of her child, when I met her, she was still so overwhelmed with joy at finally becoming a mother that she talked about it for most of the time. In telling me about her ordeal during her years of sterility, she mentioned in a matter of fact way that she had had a strong and continuous desire to kill herself, which was only suppressed due to the fear of sin associated with such an act. The way she mentioned her desire to end her life implied a belief that every woman in her place would feel the same way.

The very low status of women in the traditional Greek milieu and the idealization of motherhood were, I believe, directly related to the importance the culture attributed to children and the family. As long as the family and not the individual was the smallest viable unit, the role of mother, vital as it was for the unit's functioning, had to be stengthened with every possible support and reward. In a culture where material rewards were not available, positive moral attributes ascribed to a person by public consensus were the most valued possession, even more valuable than physical integrity. The saying goes that 'it is better to lose your one eye than your good name'. Therefore, the culture attributed the maximum honour to the mother figure in response to its social importance. In order to magnify its importance even further, every other feminine role was stripped of any prestige whatsoever. This is in contrast to a society like our own, where, for a woman, being young and beautiful is highly admired and so is being rich, or artistic, a successful scientist, or a business woman; thus, social status is distributed among several possible roles, and motherhood becomes just one acceptable role among many. Not that rural women had many choices of action, thus making it necessary for society to accentuate the difficult role of mother to lure them into it. One might stipulate instead that, because of the hardship it entailed, the social rewards were designed to stimulate the zest and motivation in the performance of the role. For, as we all know from personal experience, the greater the importance attributed to a given task the harder we try to do it well.

The high status associated with motherhood was not automatically granted, however, with the birth of a child. The first and most important step marking the transition away from the role of woman to that of mother was reached at this stage. From then on, a mother's status would increase in proportion to her children's successful development; reaching its peak after they were honourably married off. The second important step in a woman's gain of status was achieved five or six years after her marriage when she, her husband and their children moved out of her in-laws' house to set up a separate household. Within her own house the woman was absolute mistress and would no longer accept orders from anyone, not even her father or mother-in-law.

While living within the extended family, the young bride would never sit at the dinner table with the men but would just stand by while they were eating, attending to their needs and requests. Within their own separate household the whole family, man, wife and children would eat together, making of the occasion a truly collective experience. Quite often, food was placed in the middle of the table and everyone would eat from a common bowl. They would regulate their eating tempo to that of everyone else, calculating with every bite how much everyone else had had, making sure that they did not eat more than their equal share. This way of eating symbolized the collective nature of need satisfaction. In this ritual the role of the mother was purely co-ordinating, providing a model of self-negation, eating less than everybody else and offering part of her share to the one more in need; to the thinnest child, the youngest or to the one who had worked harder on that particular day. Yet with self-negation came status and honour and the satisfaction of fulfilling an important function. So important was the role of family co-ordinator in the eyes of every woman, that even today in Athens brides resent living in the same house as their mothers-in-law as is sometimes necessitated by economic and other considerations. On the other hand, they do not seem to object the presence of their father-in-law, for it is that the presence of the older woman deprives them psychologically of their function as absolute mistress of the household.

With age the status of the mother increased considerably. As a mother of honourably married sons and daughters she transcended the limitation of her sex and became the focus of her sons' co-operation within the extended family. Only she was able to mediate successfully and contain the conflicting loyalties of married brothers. In families where the grandmother was too feeble to perform her role or had died early, the co-operation between adult brothers, essential for the economic advancement of the family, was short lived (Campbell, 1964).

In most households I visited, I noticed that the grandmother's house or the corner of the yard where she usually sat was the centre of social activity for all the members of the family. Young children would play around her, they were fed there and often put to sleep there during the day. All household tasks the women could perform sitting down, like peeling vegetables or sewing, they would bring to this part of the house to be done collectively or in company.

When I asked the young mothers what could be the best possible thing that could happen to them most of them replied, seeing my children well married off: an answer that testifies to the fact that, for the rural women, the returns from the maternal role were expected to increase with age. Since the woman's identity was inseparable from that of her children, it follows that when her children reached full adult status, becoming heads of household themselves, her own status and prestige in the community increased proportionately.

B. The husband–wife relationship

In the husband–wife relationship there was little intimacy or reciprocity in the sense of a close affective give and take. The man received from his wife attention, services and care, which he in turn offered to the children directly or indirectly. But the wife made no direct claim on the husband's affection and care. The role of the woman as co-ordinator ran counter to the expression on her part of any desires, likes and dislikes, whims or fancies; just like the leader in a therapy or encounter group, she had to be alert and responsive to the moods and needs of others while keeping her own out of the picture. Even an illness which by necessity made her the recipient of care was something the traditional woman was apologetic about. Men, when speaking of their mothers, would praise their sturdiness and endurance, referring to the number of children they had produced while working hard up until the last minute, carrying water or searching the mountains for herbs and firewood.

The family's identity and its separateness from the other families in the community was embodied in the individuality of its male head. He represented the family in the outside world; his own achievements defined the social niche where the family belonged, the fame of his manliness and valiance deterred his opponents from assaulting the women of the family and stealing its property. The women were known in the community only by their husband's first name. The wife of Michael was Michalina, the wife of George was Georgaina and the children were referred to by their own Christian name jointly with that of their father's, i.e. Helen of John, Peter of Michael, etc. In order for the woman to secure the best possible representation in the community for her children and herself, she had to build her husband's public image to the best of her ability. In order to strengthen his reputation as a fierce and strong man, she adopted in public a meek and submissive attitude towards him, walking always a few steps behind him and following readily the commands which he barked at her, demonstrating in this way that he was absolute lord and master in his own household.

In the privacy of their home, the woman's attitude toward her husband was ego building. She would drop her servile attitude to attend to his needs caringly and affectionately, providing him with food and clothes and supporting him psychologically, by listening attentively to all his troubles and discussing with him in detail possible courses of action. To the children she systematically cultivated an attitude of care and respect for their father, deriving a feeling of personal pride and achievement when the father–child relationship developed to be close and loving. While interviewing the young rural mothers, I was pleasantly surprised to see the pleasure they derived in describing how much the child loved their father more than anybody else, how the two of them played together and how excited the child would become when the father came home. I had thought that since the mother had invested so much in her child she would want his/her affection for herself.

I could not at first understand the absolute identification between husband and wife, in the rural milieu, in the absence of intimacy and affective closeness. I feel it can only be understood by considering the specific social conditions traditionally prevailing in this milieu. The existing system of a self-sufficient economy called for close co-operation between all the men in an extended family and also for a division of labour which kept some of them away from home for a prolonged period of time. In any one household, a couple of men might take to the mountains joining the local 'army' of clephts* to protect the village, another man might emigrate abroad in order to increase the household income, while others would remain in the village to cultivate the land and protect the women and children. In this context a close affective bond between husband and wife would be dysfunctional, for it would tend to inhibit the man's alternatives for action away from the household and/or interfere with the smooth performance of the maternal role during the long periods of separation. But the bond that did relate man and woman, if not based on intimacy, was nonetheless founded on profound acceptance and interdependence. The man counted on the woman to raise the children who would give meaning and hope to his life and support to his old age, while the woman counted on the man for food, protection and status.

In the collective administration of family property, the interests of all members were taken into consideration but it was the man of each nucleus who represented and negotiated the interests of his wife and children. The husband's contribution to the family budget reflected on the wife's prestige

---

* Guerillas.

and position in the village community, as well as within the extended family. If a woman lost her husband, she had to depend on the charity of others in the family for her living. She had to leave her own house and move in with her in-laws for protection, regressing in terms of status to the original state of living-in bride; whereby she had to subordinate herself to her mother or sister-in-law. Seeing the budget of her in-laws shrink to provide for her and her children was a daily source of humiliation for the widow. She had to make every possible effort to contribute to the family income, by sewing and embroidering for others or keeping a few extra hens and selling the eggs for example. With the possibility of remarriage out of the question, she had to resign herself to long years of extra hard work and no social position till her own children, her sons in particular, reached adulthood and could set up their own household. 'Τὸ ὀρφανὸ δὲν χαμογελᾶ, ἡ χήρα δὲν καμαρώνει', 'The widow has nothing to take pride in, the orphan nothing to smile for' goes a village saying. Within this social reality a woman knew well enough that her husband, and he alone, could provide her and her children with the prerequisites necessary to a respectable and satisfactory life. The importance of the husband's contribution was in every way as binding to the woman as the manifestation of interpersonal intimacy.

C. The community of women

Rural women found in the company of other women all the personal intimacy and affective intensity lacking in their relationship with their husbands. Proximity between houses, homogeneity of the daily routine, shared activities and common economic interests were factors facilitating the close contact between women of all ages.

   In most rural households I visited, the young women I observed were closely surrounded by others of about the same age, mothers younger and older, unmarried girls and some old women. While married women each had their own responsibilities and their own space which they managed, the natural and social space they moved in during the day encompassed several households adjacent to one another, which women and children treated as a unified space. It was somewhat difficult for me to understand at first what was going on as I watched the continuous alternations of social and private activity around me. In between the performance of one task and another, women were seen dropping into a relative's house for a couple of minutes, exchanging a few comments about the ongoing activity and leaving without greetings or explanations. Or they might just stand around silently for a short while and then leave. Obviously, my presence in a given house, which was something of a curiosity, and the fact that my hostess could not leave while I was there to go visiting herself, tended to draw more callers into the house than would normally come in otherwise. But whatever reason each woman had for dropping into a relative's or friend's house, she never felt compelled to verbalize it, for not once did I hear anyone say 'I came here for this or that reason'. Apparently, the rural women I observed were treating each other's houses (those belonging to relatives and ingroup neighbours that is) as we treat different rooms in the same house; the transitions from one space to another and the alternation of private and social activity that they entail took place casually, briefly and repeatedly.

During the afternoons the visits tended to be more prolonged. Walking through a village, especially during the summer months, one would often see groups of women sitting together embroidering, chatting and supervising the young ones playing. Yet even at the afternoon gatherings, the comings and goings were quite frequent, bearing little resemblance to our notion of a social call. To the rural mothers, contact with other women seemed to be the 'closing sentence' of one routine event and the 'introduction' to the next; a kind of interlude designed to liven up and enrich the sequence of daily events and keep each woman in touch with those around her, their mood and their activities. Socializing was interlocked with housekeeping and child-rearing and did not constitute an independent activity alloted a special time and place.* In spite of the close contact between women, the social and emotional bonds, the daily co-operation and common interests uniting them, each woman functioned as a separate person and they did not all form an undifferentiated collective unit. Within the context of the collaboration, there was room for controlled competitiveness, criticism, gossip, individual likes and dislikes, unlimited support and mutual enrichment. While each woman bore full responsibility for her actions, her behaviour was directly and indirectly influenced by the opinion of others, their potential criticism and their example. The cleanliness of the separate houses, the appearance of the laundry as it hung out to dry, the flowers growing in front of each house, the performance of the daily tasks, the husband–wife public and semi-private behaviour, and, most importantly, the mother–child behaviour pattern constituted topics of continuous conversation among women, flavoured with praise or disapproval. The intense interaction between

---

* Only on important occasions like a name day, an engagement or a christening, did visits acquire a ceremonious character; their function then being social and not interpersonal, in the sense that they were occasions for each family to show off the range of its social connections. To this purpose, visitors put on their best clothes and sat around silently, carefully observing one another, storing up information for interfamilial discussion.

women and the continuous preoccupation with each other's performance exerted a unifying influence on women's behaviour, providing them with a sense of security for their actions and an incentive for trying their best.

The gatherings of women functioned, among other things, as an encounter group where every day individual problems were brought forward and handled by the group. However, in contrast to the artificial encounter groups emerging in large cities, which are usually organized in the context of some mental health centre meeting on set dates and cut off from the participants daily life, the encounter of rural women was a continuous every day life process which did not handle verbal accounts of problems but faced them in action. For example a young mother would be seen to drop in on the yard where other women were gathered, bringing along her toddler and his food. Without any explanation she would just sit down and start feeding him. Should the toddler object, the mother would insist and then stop. Another woman would then take over with the same food, or food from another house (such as a piece of cheese and bread, a fried potato or aubergine) would be brought forward and offered to the youngster. This whole procedure would be accompanied by a minimum of comments and would not last for more than about fifteen minutes, whereupon mother and toddler (and food) would depart, to return later in the day.

In another instance, a group of women were seen gathered around a kneading trough where one of them was about to start making bread. Before the process actually began, a lengthy discussion took place about all the details of breadmaking, with each woman offering specific suggestions about one thing and another. The person who was involved in the activity seemed to welcome all the stream of comment and advice inspite of the fact that only a small proportion of what was said genuinely influenced her behaviour. After some time spent in discussion, the other women would leave allowing the person involved in the activity to decide for herself where to place the kneading trough, how much flour to use at a time, etc. For, no matter how experienced in household tasks, a rural woman would never perform them 'automatically', without giving each time lengthy consideration to all possible alternatives of action. In this context, the advice of others was welcome for, if it did not teach anything new, at least it exposed all potential courses of action which might have skipped the person's mind.

This type of behaviour deserves further comment for it reflects, I believe, an attitude about task performance which is markedly different from the one adopted by modern urban dwellers. Contrary to the tendency of modern man to standardize, as much as possible, life's recurring activities and to organize them on the basis of a fixed day and time schedule, rural people, and women in particular, seemed to look for variation and uncertainty on every event, even the most ordinary. In fact, change and originality in the performance of routine tasks appeared to be highly encouraged and, as Miller (1958) noted, 'each event no matter how often similar ones have occurred before is viewed essentially as fresh and unique'. The time, the place and the order in which recurring activities were performed were varied with each performance. But this variety was not the result of haphazard behaviour just to break the monotonous regularity of ordinary tasks. It was essentially related to the basic outlook of rural women, who envisaged each task as an event embedded within the total frame of the household and the natural environment.

The role of the woman as a co-ordinator dictated an awareness on her part of the ever changing dynamic field of which she was a part, comprising people, animals and the elements of nature. In fact, what the rural woman needed was not just awareness but rather extreme sensitivity to minor variations in her environment in order to perform her co-ordinating role adequately, minimizing error and maximizing returns from every single event as a society of scarcity demanded of her. As a trained group leader knows, each meeting of the same group is a unique event; an intervention which may bring beneficial results one day may prove detrimental on another, and an approach which may work with one person may not work with another. The leader carefully weighs his every action against the signals received by each individual person and the group as a whole in the course of the meeting, rather than acting on a preplanned schedule. Similarly, the rural mother monitored her every activity to fit smoothly within the existing state of affairs around her, as continuously transformed by human needs and natural factors in interaction.

Perceiving the task as changeable and exploring alternative ways of performing it, was a very essential aspect of the traditional female role requirements. Being people—rather than activity—oriented, the traditional woman had to find ways of completing a task in a way that met best with people's needs; and as human needs change continuously, so must the ways of performing a task vary accordingly. If, for example, a woman had to bake bread on a day when her young child was ill and had to stay in bed, by changing the place where she kneads she could complete her task while staying near him.

It is my impression that the notion of standardization of performance which we urban dwellers tend to favour for many tasks reflects a value hierarchy, favouring the outcome over the process and the activity over the environmental field, which is the reverse from the one encountered in the rural milieu. Obviously, if one was to look only for the best possible way of performing a given task, one would come up with a rather standard procedure and place of action, but this would have to exclude from the picture environmental variation. In an urban setting and for activities where no other people are directly involved but the individual concerned, environmental factors can be assumed to be rather constant. But what about the cases where several people are directly or indirectly affected by a given activity and what about maternal role performance in particular?

Are we not led to ignore the human element, in a way, when we take for granted that cakes are only prepared in the kitchen and children only sleep in bedrooms? I cannot help thinking back as I write these lines of the many cakes I have baked for my children, giving all my attention to the details in the recipe, striving for quality in the end product, and while focusing on the task ignoring, or trying to, the very people it was supposed to serve. The differential value attributed to the process versus the outcome, the people versus the task is, I believe, at the root of many important behavioural differences I observed between the rural and urban mothers; and I might add, very much at the root of many conflicts and problems urban women encounter in their child-rearing role. This point of view will be presented more extensively in Part III, which deals with the urban mothers and their social milieu. I mention it here as well for I believe it to be a central dimension, shaping an important part of maternal behaviour.

Maternal behaviour is by definition social behaviour. If I was to summarize the research findings pertaining to the difference between the kind of institutional care which is so detrimental to the child's development and optimal maternal care, the main point I would make is that, while professional caretakers are entrusted to get the babies fed, cleaned, supervised and so on, ideally mothers are more oriented to feeding, cleaning and supervising their children, i.e. focusing on the interaction as much as on the outcome. It is very important, however, to consider whether this 'process'- and 'people'-orientation constitutes the dominant value of the social system as a whole, or whether it is an exception reserved to certain groups of people like mothers, therapists and teachers. If the dominant ideology in a given milieu runs counter to the ideology demanded of a certain role, most likely the performance of that role will be plagued by contradictions, with two sets of values dictating two forms of behaviour.

If the functioning of a given socio-economic system necessitates a predominant or exclusive task-orientation most of the social institutions will be so designed as to implicitly or explicitly reinforce this orientation. In the western world, formal education offers systematic training in this way. From nursery school onwards we are oriented to focus on the outcome of our actions and to ignore our own moods and those of others. Similarly, in most professional activities we are expected to behave likewise. Only within the context of the family, the rules of the game are expected to be reversed, or are they? And if they are, can this be done? Can the individual switch on and off value systems? After eight hours of denial or suppression of personal feelings and indifference to the state of others, can the child, returning from school and the father and mother from work, switch on their introspective and interpersonal sensitivity?

For the traditional rural Greek people no such problem existed. They lived in a people-oriented society, where interdependence was the founding stone of the entire social and economic superstructure: interpersonal intimacy, its necessary prerequisite, and all social institutions offered continuous training in this direction. For the rural mother in particular, the social institution which provided the necessary frame for the development and continuous refinement of interpersonal skills was the community of related women.

From the moment of her birth till old age, the rural woman was closely surrounded by women of all ages, with whom she shared daily life and a common predicament. Thinking back to my contact with rural women, the one thing that stands out in my memory most vividly is the scarcity of verbal exchanges and the intensity of the non-verbal ones. Observing as an outsider a gathering of women, one had the impression that most of the time there was hardly any interaction at all. Only upon entering the scene as a participant did the impact of the other women around become apparent. There were no prolonged discussions and little asking and no demanding. There was mostly parallel action monitored continuously to correspond to personal and interpersonal dispositions. When women embarked upon lengthy discussions it was usually to criticize the actions of someone who was not present.

When I developed a more intimate relationship with one of the mothers it always started in pretty much the same way. At some moment when we found ourselves alone and if we happened to sit close to one another, while we were both following the toddler in his explorations, the mother would volunteer a personal comment; briefly expressing a feeling of fatigue for example or worry over something going on that day. On the basis of my response, I suppose, she would decide whether to continue giving a personal note to our exchanges or not. In every case, however, the first personal comment was a kind of offering, exposing herself rather than asking questions. Except for the very basic questions, whether I was married and had children, no mother asked me anything about my background. It was left to me to say or show as much as I wanted of myself. It was as if the rule of interpersonal communication was 'giving' first and then 'taking' indirectly as a consequence, but not asking or demanding.

It may seem far-fetched to equate 'complaining' with 'giving' but, as I see it, in the traditional rural community the open expression of personal concerns was a form of offering. Within this social context people and their personal experiences, i.e. their ways of doing things, their efforts, errors and achievements, constituted the most valuable source of learning. Therefore, the more complete a picture each person presented of himself relating actions to feelings, the more information he was providing to those around him from which to draw from. When a woman acted in public, revealing at the same time her state of mind and her feelings, she allowed other women to share her approach fully at the objective and subjective level. When a mother brought to her neighbour's yard her child, the food he refused to eat and her consternation, it offered each of her neighbours the opportunity to survey that particular problem from a certain distance, and to rehearse cooly and to observe the results of alternative modes of action. It would not be necessary for a woman to have a child of the same age and with eating problems to benefit from the shared experience. If the child's eating is not a problem all mothers share, the feelings of fatigue, consternation, impatience related to child care certainly are. The ways of handling these feelings and expressing them in a non-disruptive and non-destructive fashion entail social skills which can improve considerably with appropriate modelling and experience. I consider the open expression of feeling among rural women to be a basic factor transforming the relationship from mere companionship to a creative experience, helping women greatly in their child rearing role.

Any one involved with children knows that optimal development depends as much on the adequate provision of food, sanitary conditions and protection from harm as on the social climate in which the give and take occurs. A child being bathed, fed or supervised by someone who is bored, tired, irritated or angry, gains much less than if the caretaker was of a more positive disposition. But negative feelings are inevitable, being part of the normal repertoire of human expression. If children are to receive optimal care, I believe mothers should have a chance of handling these feelings in ways other than ignoring, denying or associating them with guilt. In a social context where the emphasis is on achievement and personal moods are a private affair, I doubt that people are given many chances to refine their ways of handling their feelings. My experiences as a clinical psychologist have taught me that self-awareness and sincere self-expression, voiced in a way that befits the particular circumstances, are basic prerequisites to a satisfactory close interpersonal communication. Additionally, I have seen that both self-awareness and self-expression are human skills that improve with practice. For this reason, I attribute so much importance to the open expression of feeling among rural women. In as much as mothering is primarily transactional, I believe that within the context of the traditional rural community, women found the kind of human exchange necessary for the performance of the maternal role; a social context that not only tolerated but valued the expression of feeling, offering continuous opportunities of refining the modes of expression through modelling.

Within this context, a mother who happened to be irritable or angry knew that she had no reason to feel uneasy about it, since she had seen every other woman around her in a similar mood at some time or another. Secondly, by observing their behaviour, she had learned that feelings shared are easier to bear and this she had ample opportunity to do herself. Additionally, she knew what to expect of her child on such occasions and she had also seen that it would be better for both mother and child if he turned to other people around for company and stimulation on such occasions. By observing each other's total behaviour, mothers learned of ways of feeding a child when tired and irritable, for example, and of ways of handling this task when they were themselves tired and irritable. This is the kind of valuable information which no expert or manual can provide. This form of total communication, entailing a sharing of actions and feelings, presupposes a level of identification and mutual trust which we urban dwellers cannot visualize very easily. The public display of personal weakness, concerns or difficulties, successes and satisfactions, presupposes an audience that cares enough to observe and listen to the message expressed and act accordingly. For, as we all know, it can be very frustrating to express personal concerns to a deaf ear. Yet, in our pluralist society, other people's problems and complaints are usually just a burden. Loaded as we are with our personal concerns, we have little to gain from immersing ourselves in another person's experiences, which seldom correspond exactly with our own. When they do, as for example in the case of co-workers mobilized for a common cause, their interest in each other's actions and the ensuing intimacy almost automatically increases.

Within the context of the traditional extended family, the common concerns and daily experiences offered women the necessary prerequisites for mutual care and intimacy. Every woman had vested interests in the life of every other woman around her, because they were part of the same extended family or ingroup and up to a point shared the same social predicament and secondly because every event and activity that took place around her was also part of her own life and of immediate concern to her.

We are used to expressing our interest in other people by asking questions. Maybe because it is necessary that we state explicitly our willingness to shoulder even momentarily the other person's concerns. In the rural milieu the interactional process began one step ahead; starting with the implicit statement 'I trust you care enough about me and I therefore tell you of my worries'. Questions were not asked for they would be forcing the other person to talk before he was ready to do so. In this context questionnaires used by social scientists can cause quite some embarrassment. All of us who have worked with rural Greek people have known that country people are not very comfortable with questionnaires and tend to give very guarded brief answers. Intuitively, after the pilot study I conducted, I concluded that the questionnaire had to be very short and ought to be administered at the end of the three-day visits after we had established some rapport with our subjects. Today, after my recent experience, I would abolish it altogether if possible. For I believe that the differences between the urban and the traditional rural way of life are so fundamental that the brief responses can only yield very superficial information. To me the most meaningful experiences, which helped me understand, feel and momentarily share the rural people's reality, occurred mostly outside the frame of the structured observation or the interview.

The one time I really penetrated the community of women was through a very unorthodox route (for a scientist at least), but it proved to be the only way for me to gain the women's acceptance, to be treated as one of them and offered a first hand experience of what sharing means in this context and how it works.

In one of the households I visited, one in which the network of related women appeared unusually large and active, the prominent figure appeared to be an older aunt, a woman of about 55 years of age. As she came and went several times in the course of the two hours we spent in the yard during the first visit, I noticed that almost all the women who happened to be around each time she came over had a comment to exchange with her; a sign that she held a prominent position in the community. When I was offered coffee, she suggested that I drink it with her at her house for she could read the future in the coffee cup. I thanked her for her offer and told her that I would gladly have her read my future but that we would have to wait until after the observational visits. She looked at me, straight in the face, smiled vaguely and made no further comment. I was not quite sure whether I had offended her or not, but since I had no other choice (Methodology über alles!) I considered the matter closed and didn't give it a second thought.

On the last visit, during the mid-morning break, when the mother I was observing brought me the traditional spoonful of jam, she said she had not made coffee for me that day since I would be drinking it at Aunt Tassia's. Half an hour before the end of my last observational session, Aunt Tassia came in and sat quietly in the yard knitting. By the time I had finished observing and I was packing my timer and notepad, I was well aware that within the community of women Aunt Tassia was taken quite seriously and so was her fortune-telling. I was also aware that everybody around had taken for granted the fact that I would be visiting her on that day and would have my own future read out. What I did not know at the time was that I was myself responding quite seriously to Aunt Tassia and her offer. The house where she lived alone was one of the most modest I had visited, but was extremely clean, neat and over-ornated with lace mats, lace curtains, lace sofa covers and bedspreads. When I arrived , she immediately made me coffee and as soon as I had finished it she turned the cup upside down, left it standing for a few minutes and then examined it intently for a while.* She made a couple of brief comments of a general nature about my past life which were rather appropriate and then after a long pause she said, 'as for your one and all important problem I see that the road to its solution is a long and hard one and right at the start there is a large stumbling block.' I did have a major problem at the time, which I believed I had left temporarily behind me in Athens. I did not know I was carrying it with me during my field work, I did not know it was troubling me all the time, all I do know is that as soon as I heard this statement tears filled my eyes. Although she appeared to be focusing on the coffee cup, Tassia noticed my emotion and stopped the fortune-telling to make a personal supporting comment. I cannot recall exactly what was said, but I do remember that I found myself quite naturally telling her of the matter, of which I seldom if ever talked about. She in turn, instead of offering advice, asking for details or commenting on what I had told her, simply told me very briefly her own life story; the story of an unusually tormented life.

During the civil war she and her husband had joined the Democratic army. After the defeat, when the exodus to the Eastern bloc began in fear of retaliations, she had to stay behind to look after her newly born child. Her husband left and she returned to the village where the family refused to accept her, fearing the political 'stigma' she carried with her. She was allowed to live in the family barn in semi-isolation and had to work as best as she could to support herself and her child. She did not tell me how she managed, she only showed me her lace work which had been, over the last few years, her main source of income. Seeing the status she enjoyed among women thirty years later, I knew she had achieved the impossible.

The impact of a living example is very great indeed, much greater I think than the best advice, for I recall that when I left Tassia's house the seriousness of my problem, in comparison to what I had heard, appeared considerably smaller. It was then that I realized how handicapped we are when we try to solve our personal problems relying exclusively on our own experiences as our only frame of reference. At some level of abstraction, Tassia's problem and my own had a common core despite the total difference in specifics. There was much for me to learn even from the brief narration. The calmness of her voice, tinted with occasional sadness at the reminder of the pain she had suffered and pride for the outcome of her struggles, was a

---

* The type of coffee usually drunk in Greece forms a thick sediment of muddy texture at the bottom of the cup. When the cup is turned upside down the sediment covers the inside of the cup forming Rorschach type patterns.

source of encouragement to me, building my hopefulness for human endurance and resourcefulness. I left her house thinking very dearly of her and
filled with admiration for the adjustive capacity of a woman who had been
condemned to near death for her rebellion (social and political) and yet
managed not only to survive but eventually to assert herself. Capitalizing on
her sensitivity, undoubtedly sharpened by solitude, fear for the future, pain
and anger for the injustice she was suffering, she managed to regain access
to the community that had ostracized her. She transformed her predicament
as a peripheral person to that of a different or even exceptional one, who
could offer others something no one else could, a glimpse into the future
(whether real or imaginary it is of little importance at this point).

When Tassia and I returned to the mother's house where I had left my
things, the signs of a vivid experience must still have been apparent on my
face for, to the enquiring eyes of the two women who were there, Tassia
murmured almost inaudibly 'she has her own troubles too', 'ἔχει καὶ αὐτή τά
βάσανά της'. The mother I was observing urged me to stay on a little longer.
She made two cups of coffee and sat next to me so we could drink it together.
All the other times she had just made coffee for me and had continued with
her housework while I was drinking it, making a comment now and then as
she was coming and going. On that occasion she sat silently for a while
focusing exclusively on the interaction. The child was somewhere else with
the grandmother and we were just four women in the room, sitting silently
yet comfortably (Aunt Tassia, the mother, a neighbour and myself). The
mother broke the silence saying, 'I did not know that women in Athens had
troubles too,' she paused for a while and then added, 'I guess on every door
there is a nail', 'ὅπου πόρτα καί καρφί'. I made a general remark about the
difficulties of urban living and after that we began a slow exchange of
comments interpolated with frequent pauses. The fourth woman who up to
that point had had little personal contact with me sat silently for a while,
hesitating to join in the personal conversation. She then got up and left
without a word to reappear a couple of minutes later bringing some cookies.
'I made them yesterday, they go well with coffee,' she said putting some on
the table and giving me a small bagful to take away, and then joined in the
conversation. Probably to the three rural women this whole exchange was a
rather ordinary event, to me it was extraordinary and even overwhelming. I
drank my coffee and left with a clear notion that the taste of life when shared
fully with others is distinctly different from that lived in pursuit of independence and solitary achievement.

4   Infancy and Childhood in Traditional Rural Villages

In the pages that follow I shall attempt to give a picture of what it meant to be a child in a rural Greek village. Moving gradually from infancy to childhood, I hope to illustrate the opportunities available within this particular setting for the satisfaction of children's social needs.

The picture I attempt to draw is based, however, on rather uneven informational material. Although my extensive involvement with the rural Greek milieu has provided me with a wealth of information about children's daily lives, the only age group I have observed systematically are the 15–17-month-olds. The mothers I observed systematically were chosen to have only one child, and although most of them were expecting their second child, none had actually had a second baby at the time of the observation. For the 15–17-month-olds my observation encompassed both the private and public domain—since I stayed in the house while the children were fed, dressed and sometimes put to sleep. However, I saw mostly the public behaviour of the younger and older children when they came into the house or yard where I was observing, carried by their mothers or on their own. In some cases, I had a chance to observe parts of the daily routine of a baby or an older child living in the household I was observing or in a neighbouring one. Nonetheless, the fact remains that I have more or less objective facts only for the toddlers, while for the other age groups the information I have is mostly of an impressionistic nature.

A. The infants

The birth of a baby in a rural Greek household was a major event and cause for great joy for the entire family, especially in the case of a couple's first child. It was the main event for which the man and woman had been preparing for all their lives.

The first forty days of his life the baby would spend almost exclusively in his mother's arms. A whole array of superstitions was activated to prevent the mother from stepping outside her house during this period. After childbirth, a woman was said to be particularly vulnerable to the spell of the evil eye and was said to be an agent of bad luck to any household she might visit. She thus had to stay at home, responding to the child's every demand. For a couple of weeks the mother stayed in bed with the baby by her side. Since women after childbirth go through a period of increased sensitivity, we may suppose that the prolonged physical contact between mother and baby did set the ground for mutual signal detection and helped the mother tune in with the baby's rhythm.

When the mother no longer needed to stay in bed, the baby was placed during the daytime in a small rocking cradle carved out of wood.* Once there he would pass for a while to the care of the grandmother, who, while sitting and spinning wool, would rhythmically rock the cradle with her foot singing occasionally. Quite naturally, all the adults of the household and the older children took care not to disturb the baby's sleep, not to frighten him with loud noises or to over-excite him with stimulation. Men, women and children were seen keeping their voices down when a baby was asleep, or standing near him while he was awake in his mother's arms, looking at him for quite a while smiling and just whispering to him.

As long as the baby was healthy, he was considered to be a blessing to the family. I only ever heard comments of a positive nature about a baby in a rural household. All new developments in his behavioural repertoire were discussed among relatives as sure signs of intelligence and strength. A colicky baby, who might keep the entire family sleepless for several nights, was considered to be under the spell of the evil eye; thus the relatives were compensated for their suffering by the 'knowledge' that their tiny kinsman was so special as to become the object of envy for an outgroup person.

Up to about the age of four, a child was considered to be a creature who could not reason and therefore could not benefit from training and punishment. The notion of spoiling a baby, especially during the first two years of life, appeared to be inconceivable to the rural mothers I met. Their attitude was that the best thing they could do for their child's future development was to meet his every need as well as their means allowed. In the rural Greek milieu, as the most valuable means were the human resources available, rural mothers welcomed any assistance offered by relatives and grandparents in particular. Babies of over five-months-old, but prior to the age

---

* These wooden cradles called 'sarmenitsa' are now collectors' items, for in their simplicity they are often remarkable examples of popular craftmanship.

when they began walking, could be seen using their grandmother's lap as their playpen. They would sit more or less quietly with their back against her facing towards the room and either interact with another person or play with a household object. When restless, the baby would be carried around and shown various items in the environment which he was allowed to fondle at will. Breakable objects were hidden away, so as not to trigger the baby's interest and provoke frustration.

In all households I visited I was told that the toddler I was observing had been swaddled for at least five months. Immediately after birth the baby was swaddled like a mummy, with hands wrapped tightly next to his body, and was held in this position all day and night. The ritual of unwrapping the swaddling band, which reportedly occurred with varying frequency from one baby to another, was a lengthy and intricate one. The unwrapping and wrapping of the band(s) and the period of time the baby spent in freedom in between appeared to constitute the highlight of the mother–infant interaction (except breastfeeding of course) during the first couple of months of a baby's life. The mother unwrapped the swaddling cloth very very slowly, looking at the baby's face almost continuously, stopping every now and then to let him kick and stretch, talking to him and keeping her body quite close to the baby's. This ritual like every other activity performed by rural people had no fixed sequence of events; it could precede or follow feeding or it might be interrupted halfway through and the baby fed while he could move his body freely. As the baby began to spend longer hours awake, the type of swaddling changed; leaving first the arms free and restricting the legs only, it was gradually omitted altogether during the day.

Despite the negative attitude we modern urban dwellers might have towards any practice that restricts so absolutely an individual's freedom of movement, there were no apparent signs in any of the toddlers I observed that swaddling had any negative effects on their development.* Possibly swaddling, when practiced in a climate of intense care and interpersonal sensitivity, coupled with rocking, singing and social interaction, works like a soothing stimulation; just another form of continuous stimulation of the kind found by Brackbill *et al.* (1966) to have beneficial effects on newly born infants.

After the age of five or six months and until he began walking the baby spent the greatest part of the time he was awake in somebody's arms, usually the mother's or the grandmother's. If the grandmother was vigorous enough to help with the housework, the mother would devote most of her time to the

---

* Dorothy Lee (1960) arrived at the same conclusion after careful observation of rural Greek children in various parts of the country.

baby, if not the roles might be partly reversed. In the case of a firstborn child, however, the mother's eagerness to assert herself in her new role was so great that she would go to great pains to complete her housework while the baby was asleep, in order to look after him herself when awake. As a rule, the mother of a newly born baby, known as the 'moromana' (μωρομάνα), would stay at home for almost an entire year after the baby's birth, attending to the housework and the baby's needs and leaving outside work to the other members of the family. But if a pressing need for extra help in the fields did arise, the 'moromana' would strap a splint or the wooden cradle, with the baby in it, on her back and take to the fields. Once there, she would hang the splint or cradle from a tree, to keep the baby away from animals and reptiles, and work in the fields, returning to the baby every now and then to breast-feed him.

The rural people's pronounced interpersonal orientation, their skills in non-verbal communication, the slow and steady pace in which women completed their daily tasks, the presence within the household of women and children of different ages and, most importantly, the significance the culture attributed to children were all factors resulting in a setting highly conducive to the satisfaction of infant needs. The presence of a grandmother, with few other demands on her time and with the wisdom of having experienced the development of over a dozen other children, a woman at the peak of her social prestige and self satisfaction, must have been particularly beneficial to a baby's first social explorations. I have of course been describing here the optimal conditions, which we can assume existed for some of the rural people some of the time. Lest I appear over-idealistic about the conditions prevailing in the traditional rural Greek villages, I should note that crises were a frequent part of life and when they did occur they demanded added effort on the part of both men and in particular women, who under normal circumstances were already overworked. Yet even under conditions of hardship, every effort was made to spare the infants from experiencing the negative circumstances. This effort was made not only by parents, close relatives and ingroup members, but even unrelated neighbours would offer food, clothing and even temporary shelter to babies of needy families.

B. The toddlers

For rural children, beginning to walk marked their first move away from the exclusive care of the immediate family and towards other adults and children around the house. This they did under their mother's continuous observation. Toddlers spent most of their waking time in the same space as their mothers, either in the house or in the yard. Most of this time they were interacting with her. The interaction with the mother at this age, however, was not absorbing all the child's energy. Rather, the mother was used as a secure base or a stable point of reference from which the toddler explored the environment. He might hold the mother's hand to walk around when his pace was not very stable, or he might sit next to her while fondling a household object, he would turn to look at her every now and then as he trotted away or played with someone else, and might bring back to her a new discovery. In many instances it was the mother who initiated the interaction, offering the child something to eat or play with, changing his course when it appeared to her that he was heading towards danger, picking him up when he fell, talking to him, smiling and caressing him.

Most of the time a child was awake there were people around him, apart from his mother, for whom he was the centre of attention. When rural people sit together they seldom chat. Usually they talk when they have something specific to communicate to one another. They may argue fiercely and at length when there is a difference of opinion, but they also may remain silent for quite a while carefully observing the other people around them. In my presence—which tended to minimize personal discussions—adults visiting each other's house just sat together almost silently, their attention focused on the most mobile element in the environment, i.e. the toddler(s) trotting about. Some adults might initiate some form of interaction with the child, but most would play with, talk to, or caress him only when the child made some form of advance to them. I was surprised to see in some cases ten or twelve adults in the same place all interacting with one 15-month-old child without irritating him; for their responsive attitude usually resulted in one adult interacting with the child at a time, however briefly. In this way human contact, abundant as it was, helped to sharpen the child's perceptual abilities without overwhelming him.

Rural children spent their waking time involved with 'play' objects, interacting with their mother, interacting with other people, satisfying physical needs and moving from one place to another. In general terms their activities did not differ markedly from those of most 15-month-olds the world over. The main differences I noted from my experience with urban children were the absence of toys and the type of interaction children had with adults. Toddlers' manipulation of objects was likely to include exploration of items in the environment, i.e. door knobs, chairs, tables, tablecloths, flowers, leaves, bugs, feathers, animals, people's clothing and mechanical equipment, like tractors, motorcycles, etc. The number of actual toys available was minimal, including mostly small plastic toys usually found in potato chip bags and detergents. The few large size toys seen in these households were mostly dolls, which were placed high up on a shelf as a decoration item and were never seen to be fondled by children. Children did not seem to be given objects, i.e. toys, for their own exclusive use. This attitude was not only the result of poverty but was also dictated by a lack of need. Rural children were seldom seen playing alone. The periods of time they did spend alone were particularly brief. People and the natural environment with all the stimulation it provided were the children's real life 'play things'. On the basis of quantity alone, human interaction was clearly the central component of the child's daily activity. When we speak of socialization in the rural Greek milieu we speak of a process that taught the young child to live in very close proximity to several other people for a prolonged period of time; a process that taught a child to be social indeed.

Gradually changing the priorities of his attachments and expanding the circle of the important others, the growing child had at all ages a group of people around him who knew him intimately and with whom the interaction was well suited to his own needs. The toddler's social group usually consisted of the mother and father, grandparents, if they were still vigorous, a couple of school age girl cousins, aunts with young children, unmarried aunts and uncles and the grandparents' friends and neighbours, especially those who did not have young grandchildren of their own. If the grandparents were not strong enough to put in the effort required for the supervision of a vivacious toddler, they confined themselves to the care of infants and story-telling to older children.

As the child passed from infancy to toddlerhood and his need and tolerance for intense stimulation increased, the role held at first by the grandmother was gradually taken over by the father. In most of the households I visited, the children's most noticeable attachment was to their fathers as compared to other relatives.* Most fathers upon their return from work, either during the day for a lunch break or at the end of the day, first turned to their child; they would carry him about, fondle him, talk to him, occupying themselves with the child for quite a while before sitting down to eat. The children, upon their father's appearance, would show such signs of delight, often presenting an amusing sight as they shouted and yelled, lifting their arms to be picked up and stumbling over objects in their effort to get near him. Fathers spent quite some time with boys in particular. If they had any kind of vehicle they would often take their sons for rides; they might even be seen holding a 15-month-old boy on the saddle of a motorcycle or a tractor, pretending to teach him how to drive it and allowing the child to touch and explore every part of it. During the afternoon hours, some fathers

---

* The comparison does not include the mother. Since the mothers did not leave their child for any prolonged period of time while I was in the house.

occasionally took their 15-month-old son with them to the local café (καφενείο)—as did some grandfathers as well, keeping the child there for as long as he appeared to enjoy it.

It is no exaggeration, I think, to say that rural children discovered the world through other people. During the first four years of a child's life, the extended family and the ingroup formed a social ring around him, which was at the same time protective and stimulating. Each person would offer of himself his time and experience to satisfy the child's exploratory drive; each making his own unique contribution. In one instance I saw a grandmother holding her 15-month-old grandson on one knee and on the other one of her own live hens for the child to explore safely and at will. In another case I recall a middle aged woman placing her 16-month-old nephew on a kitchen table and her two highschool age daughters on both sides of it to keep the child from falling off while she cleaned artichokes for dinner, giving the child the fuzz and leaves to play with and watching carefully his every move.

Rarely if ever were adults seen playing with young children on equal terms with them, indulging that is in childlike activities like playing ball, building blocks, etc. This the children did with other children of the same age or older. From adults they took what only they could give, i.e. their experience, which was translated into increased opportunities for the growing child for safe exploration. This kind of adult–child interaction presupposed, on the part of the adult, full knowledge of the environmental stimuli and their potential dangers, equally good knowledge of the particular child and his abilities and continued attention in order to keep the child's activities always within safety limits. Therefore, this kind of adult–child interaction outside the immediate family would only be possible in a setting allowing adults and children close daily contact.

In the rural Greek milieu I believe that it was not only proximity that facilitated the adult–child interaction; proximity is a necessary condition for smooth interaction, but it is not the only prerequisite. In the case of the rural people, their attitude towards work and human interaction appeared to be the key factor. In the traditional collective way of life men and in particular women worked for the family, carrying out their daily tasks with the welfare of others in mind. There was no notion of a task fulfilled for its own sake or for self-satisfaction. All activity had a purpose and the purpose was social. Inasmuch as individuality was an alien concept, people were not evaluated by their actions in abstract, but by the social repercussions of their actions. A promiscuous daughter was accused of dishonouring the family. A good housewife was not praised for the quality of her cuisine, but for the health and weight of her children. A talented builder was not esteemed for the beautiful houses he constructed, but for the number of people he had pleased through his work and the large ingroup he had acquired. Thus a person in any kind of work had to keep his attention tuned to the stimuli coming in from the people around him, since it was for them that he worked and they were the all important judges of the outcome. Traditional people did not withdraw or isolate themselves to complete a task; they were trained to focus both on the task at hand and the social environment. Thus toddlers, in their insatiable need for human contact, would find in almost any adult in their environment someone ready to respond to their social call; someone that is who could become involved in an interpersonal exchange without acting in anyway out of the ordinary.

C. Age four and beyond

During infancy and early childhood, while the child was quite dependent on adult care for the satisfaction of his needs, all the related adults around the rural child played the role of the caretaker, providing stimulation, protection, food and shelter as necessary. As the child reached the age when he needed a certain amount of independence, in order to develop a sense of autonomy and initiative, the role of the social entourage was not reduced, but appropriately transformed instead. Children over the age of four received from the adults near them not only nurturance but training as well in specific skills and in desirable attitudes. This was achieved informally through communal living, as the daily life of adults and children of all ages was closely entangled and intimately interrelated.

Passing from one age bracket to the next entailed for the rural children—as for all people for that matter—certain changes in the composition of their social group. With age the importance of the peer group as a socializing agent increased and interestingly enough so did the importance of the outgroup. The organization of the village area into friendly and unfriendly households was in itself a factor facilitating autonomous exploration; for the contrasting forces gave the young child a feeling of security that eased exploration and a sense of threat that kept him constantly on his guard. When a 4-year-old child ran an errand half an hour's distance away from home, as he walked towards his destination, his home was not the only secure base from which he had to move further and further away. He had instead a couple of minutes' walk to make to the first relative's house and from there another few minutes to the next friend's house and still another short distance to cover to another familiar house and so on until he had covered the entire 30 minute distance. In this way a very young child could expand his range of exploration considerably while minimizing the danger involved. In fact, he could explore almost the entire village while remaining within easy reach of assistance from a caring adult.

If, on the other hand, an exaggerated sense of self confidence and the spirit of adventure took a young child beyond the protection of his own people, he was almost certain to meet with some maltreatment—albeit minor usually—at the hands of older unrelated children and with verbal harrassment from unrelated adults. Among outgroup families even young children were treated with suspicion and guarded hostility, for they were viewed as potential intruders who would reveal family secrets and weaknesses to unfriendly ears. Rightly so, for a young child's first demonstration of family spirit was to report home all he had seen concerning people outside the family and its circle of friends; while one of his prime obligations was to keep family secrets.

The hostile behaviour of the outgroup must have had a galvanizing and ego building effect on the growing child, for it was proof that despite his tender age he presented that much of a threat to people outside the family as to arouse their hostility. At the same time the threat of gossip—malevolent gossip at that, if seen misbehaving by outgroup people—must have had quite a controlling influence on children's behaviour when on their own. Thirdly it indirectly strengthened children's identification with their own family. Next to the harshness of the outgroup, the relatives' concern and tolerance did become more apparent and so did the dangers that lay waiting outside the family circle. This added awareness of the importance of the family came at a time when the child's age called for a more demanding and less tolerant attitude towards him on the part of parents and relatives. Past the age of four the child would make his first attempts to shoulder some of the family tasks; he would run errands and eagerly join in any household activity that did not demand skill or strength.

When they did run errands away from home, children usually went in groups of three or four together. But whether alone or in company, rural children were hardly ever inclined to defy adult, i.e. parental, authority. When in a group, children were quite often seen helping each other complete some adult assigned task. Or when they just played together they usually did so near their house, where they were subject to adult supervision, exposed to friendly support and protected from unfriendly criticism. When young children helped grown-ups they usually did so on their own initiative or in response to a slight hint on the part of the adults. The eagerness of young rural children to make themselves useful is something that one must see to believe. Not once did I see or hear an adult press a child to perform a task. As a rule adults did not give orders or verbal intructions to children and when they did they did not seem to expect to be obeyed absolutely. The youth who had to be ordered about in order to perform what was expected of him was considered most inadequate.

Any person of any age was expected to observe the activity that concerned him, assimilate it, decipher its rationale and repeat the activity himself through his own initiative when necessary, duly modified to suit the circumstances. The proof of the learning was in the doing; if the performance was inadequate the child might be plainly told that he had acted stupidly and, depending on the circumstances, he might be denied the opportunity to try again for a while in order to have the opportunity to do some more observing. If the child was allowed to stay on the job this was proof he was doing fine. Girls helping their mother with housework and boys joining the men, learned the adult tasks through observation, trial and error, and without instructions or explanations.

In one instance, for example, a young boy of about eight years of age was helping his father and uncles fish. The men were pulling the nets from the sea and the boy was observing intensively, while doing little things here and there, like throwing sea-weed and stones back into the sea, putting the fish that got away from the nets in a bucket, etc. At some point, some problem arose and the pulling of the nets became particularly hard. The boy cautiously moved up to where the men were standing, placed himself in line right in front of his father and began pulling as well. He worked along with the others for about 10–15 minutes and then his father, without any word of explanation, brushed the boy aside and took his place. The boy's expression did not appear to change as he moved away; there were no visible signs of disappointment or questioning. It was obvious to him that he had done as much as he could do well or as much as was needed, he thus returned to the simpler yet necessary tasks he had been doing before.

The smooth working relations between adults and children during their apprenticeship were very much the result, I think, of the intimacy and basic trust children developed for the adults they worked with over the years. Also, they were greatly facilitated by the emphasis the culture attributed to observation. By carefully observing adult behaviour, children would come to sense what needed to be done on each occasion and also by observing they would eventually figure out how it was done; thus minimizing the need for orders and commands, avoiding the risk of power struggles and developing their own initiative. Interestingly enough, the one behaviour for which young children were systematically trained was observing or 'paying attention'. Accusations of stupidity, which were quite frequently flung at children (albeit tenderly in the form of a question rather than statement), were mostly on account of inattention and rarely, if ever, on account of clumsiness due to age.

The whole pattern of communication, the lack of instructions and demands coupled with the expectation of appropriate action rested on continued intense observation. Yet, to someone accustomed to a predominantly verbal mode of interaction, this emphasis on keeping in tune with the social environment without the need for words may seem paradoxical. Dorothy Lee in her travels throughout Greece noted (1966) the case of a group of mothers with pre-school age children who had gone visiting and after a while got up and left the house without notifying the children. After they had walked a couple of yards away they began shouting at the children accusations of stupidity and inattention. This seemed to her a most unfair behaviour on the part of the mothers, who scolded the children for staying behind instead of blaming themselves for 'failure to communicate' their intention. To her, as to all of us urban dwellers, a message not communicated verbally was not communicated at all.

From several instances I observed, I formed the impression that rural Greek people not only valued non-verbal communication signals more than the verbal ones, but they actually mistrusted the verbal ones. They deliberately trained their children not to respond to a verbal message unquestioningly; that is not to act immediately but to take time to consider its soundness on the basis of other converging information. Several times I heard mothers and other adults tease young children by giving them impossible instructions like 'go and see if I am coming' or at midday 'go and see if the moon is coming out'. If the child started to go everybody laughed but if he refused, protesting at the unsoundness of the statement, he was praised for his cleverness.

The easy life ended for rural children around the age of six when they went to school. From that age onwards children were treated like responsible members of the family group; they were expected to play a representative role outside the family and to contribute to the common effort as much as possible.

School going was in itself quite a trial for rural children. Not only did they have to become involved in a type of activity for which they were totally unprepared, but they were expected to be good at it; for their performance at school—as everywhere else—reflected on the whole family. At the end of the day the school teacher would discuss at the καφενείο the children's achievements and blunders, causing the respective fathers and relatives to feel pride or shame. In the case of derogatory comments the father, as the one person responsible for matters outside the home, had to discipline his children in a way that put considerable strain on a small boy or girl. He or she was spanked and accused of misrepresenting the family and lowering its prestige, and this was repeated with almost every negative comment the teacher made about the child. Usually, in the case of children who did not do well at school, this ordeal would last for a year or two and then the family would decide that he or she was not versed for learning. In the case of a boy, he would be allowed to go to work instead, helping the adults in their daily tasks, joining from that early an age the hard life of farmer, shepherd or fisherman.

5 The Mother–Child Interaction

The principle of order and frugality characterizing the traditional rural Greek culture was reflected in the mother–child interaction. The absence of haphazard or superfluous activity and the purposefulness of all action were the dominant characteristics of the mothers' behaviour towards their children. To the casual onlooker, the ongoings in a typical household might appear to entail little interaction between mother and child. Yet by staying in the household for any length of time one gradually came to sense a very intense interaction indeed, albeit a limited activity.

Speaking of intense inter*action* in the absence of *action* may seem paradoxical. It is certainly difficult for me to describe what I sensed in the rural households without referring to nebulous concepts. The image that comes to mind that may be helpful in clarifying the seeming paradox is that of a hunter lying in ambush, waiting for the prey to come by. Although totally immobile, his state of preparedness and vigilance for any sign of the prey may be considered as much part of the hunting as the brief interludes of shooting. Similarly, the principal characteristics of the maternal behaviour I observed was this state of continuous vigilance.

From the day of their birth until the time they were mature enough to move safely outside the home boundaries, rural children were under their mother's constant supervision. Although it is quite obvious that a young child, especially during the age when he first begins to walk alone, will need continuous supervision, there is something about the quantity and quality of this supervision as exercised by rural Greek mothers which was typical, I thought, of that specific milieu and its culture.

Clarke-Stewart in the United States, just like myself in Athens and the Greek countryside, noted that mothers of 15–19-month-olds spent about 85 per cent of the time the child was awake in the same room. The proximity between mother and child at this age appears to be a universal phenomenon dictated by security reasons; if left unsupervised the child will most certainly hurt himself. Yet, while the American working class mothers spent 30 per cent of this time actually interacting with their child, for the Greek mothers the interaction time went up to 70 per cent. In practice, this increased mother–child interaction was the result of the mother's continuous pre-occupation with the child. The time intervals when she was involved with something else constituted many short interludes in the day long interaction. The mothers were seldom, if ever, seen engrossed in an activity demanding their undivided attention for a prolonged period of time while the child was awake. Demanding tasks were usually completed while the child was still asleep. The routine housework was completed at the same time as child supervision, in a continuous alternation of attention or actual comings and goings from the child to the task; with the mother usually walking away or focusing her attention elsewhere only when she saw that the child was engrossed in a safe activity that was likely to keep his interest for a while. This was inspite of the presence of several other adults in the same space, all looking after the child almost as carefully as the mother.

The impression I formed from the rural mothers I observed was that, as long as the child was young and depended on them for his survival, he was constantly the centre of their attention and his needs were given priority over everything else. While a 15-month-old child played and explored the environment, his mother would stand near him almost motionless following with her eyes his every move. She would interrupt her watch every now and then for very short intervals to attend to some household task. The single most frequent maternal behaviour in the rural milieu was looking at the child in an intense and almost continuous way. This continuous observation constituted a baseline interaction; a kind of statement of availability in practice. Careful observation preceded all other maternal behaviour, with action only coming as a response to something the child did. In this way, maternal behaviour was mostly responsive in nature and, except for brief instances when the mother deliberately interrupted the child's activity by physically removing him from potential danger, her activity blended with that of the child's and was almost unnoticeable.

The overall pattern of mother–child interaction, as already mentioned, appeared to be steady, smooth and almost continuous. Outward manifestations of tenderness like hugging and kissing were rather infrequent on the mother's part and even more infrequent were any outbursts of irritation like scolding or spanking the child. Physical contact initiated by the mother usually had a facilitating purpose; either holding the child by the hand to steady his steps, or carrying him about towards a desired object, or offering the child the opportunity to hold on to her to pull himself up. Similarly, the mother's verbal behaviour was mostly responsive in nature. Not that the mother actually answered the 15-month-old's speech, but most, if not all, of her verbal comments were directly related to the child's activity, his vocalization or his emotional state. She would sooth him when fretting, instruct him about future action, label items in his immediate environment, etc.

The most interesting form of speech, however, which was used with surprising frequency, was an ecouragement to the child to repeat what he was already doing. I believe that this type of verbal instruction is a culture specific behaviour. This behaviour pattern appeared rather perplexing to both observers (my assistant and myself) for it was deemed superfluous. The mothers appeared to be instructing their child to perform a task which he was performing anyway. For example, to a child pushing a carton box or a door the mother would say, 'push it Johnny, push it'. This form of apparently superfluous encouragement was repeated again and again following most of the child's exploratory undertakings. Possibly because this maternal behaviour is not common in other parts of the world (and for this reason was not included in the instrument developed by Clarke-Stewart), or maybe because it appeared to me quite paradoxical, I have given it some thought. And the more I thought about it the more I saw it fit the socializing role of the traditional rural mother; the role she ascribed to herself and the expectations she had of her child. If the mother just stood by while the child did 'his own thing'—as it seemed to my urban mind the 'natural' thing to do—intervening only when the child ran into some danger, she would be loading the interaction all during the child's exploratory activity with mostly negative exchanges. The rural mothers appear to have found a way of counter-balancing prohibition with positive encouragement, by instructing the child to continue a safe activity; an activity which he was most likely to repeat anyway, given young children's natural inclination for repetitive behaviour. In this way, while remaining true to their supportive role, they became a partner in the child's explorations adding the pleasure of social reward to the excitement of exploration; socializing the child to view the pleasure of discovery and achievement as something that is shared and not savoured in solitude. If this particular maternal behaviour seemed paradoxical and superfluous to me, this may well be due to the fact that it reflects a fundamental difference between independent-minded people and inter-dependent-oriented ones. While we expect our children to act on their own whenever possible and like it, people used to an interdependent way of life appear to view activity of any kind as inseparable from human interaction.

As far as prohibitions aimed to protect the child from harm were concerned, these usually took the form of very brief and effective interventions on the mother's part, which closed the issue in the shortest possible time. If, for example, a child went near a puddle, the mother would quickly go and pick him up and transport him elsewhere. On the way, she would make a brief statement about the possibility of getting wet, but the words were simply an accompaniment to a *fait accompli*. The child was given no warning about the imminent danger and no chance to disregard the warning. If the child insisted on returning to the prohibited place, he was simply removed again and presented with an alternative activity to distract his attention. If a couple of attempts failed, however, the mother would take more drastic measures like taking the child inside the house and closing the door to keep him away from the puddle until he forgot about it. To the child's protests or cries she would respond with yet another offer of distraction, without seeming to resent the insistence. At no time did I see a prohibition turn into a power struggle between mother and child. Prohibitions were not set for educational purposes; they were dictated by immediate necessity. The mother took it upon herself to enforce the prohibition while granting the child the right to try and bypass it by all means available to him, since he was too young to reason and understand the rationale behind it.

Only after the age of four was the child expected to begin to understand the cause of events. From this age onwards, if a child damaged a household item or hurt himself he was scolded for it and accused of stupidity, but he was judged mainly by the end result of his actions and was not expected to obey faithfully all instructions. If, for example, a child was warned that by climbing a certain tree he was likely to fall down and hurt himself and he went ahead and climbed it disregarding the instructions, he would be scolded only if he hurt himself, not just for disobeying.

As children grew older, mothers' supervision naturally decreased and so did the time mother and child spent together. Yet the mother's role remained basically the same over the years; children spent progressively more time outside the house, but she remained available at all times to provide nurture, support and encouragement whenever needed. Her importance in the life of her children, instead of diminishing with age, remained unchanged, for the harder they toiled at school and at work the more they came to appreciate her support. Whatever hurt or pain a child met with, he turned to his mother for comfort. Even when the father spanked the child she, without challenging his authority for a moment or denying the wrong doing, would take the child close to her and silently comfort him, assuring him of her unconditional acceptance.

In such cases as the child's misbehaviour was likely to exasperate the mother to the point where she would be likely to spank him herself quite harshly, the other women around her would intervene and actively protect both mother and child from an exaggerated outburst of anger. When Kostas, who was ten years old, failed to return home for lunch one day, having fallen asleep in a corner of an amusement park which had temporarily settled in the village, his mother fell deep in despair fearing the worst for her child. When late in the afternoon he finally woke up and started for his home, he was seen by friends and relatives who ran ahead of him to inform his mother that he was well and on his way back. Then all her anxiety turned to anger for the unnecessary torment she had endured and she began shouting, calling him names and threatening to beat him to death. In a moment several women and children had gathered around her to soothe her, telling her both how justified her anger was and how usual it is for children that age to forget themselves. While this was going on at Kostas' house, an elderly aunt living next door took the child, who had just got back and was in a state of panic, to her own house to spend the night. Knowing that this was the best solution for all concerned, the mother and father did not argue with the person who informed them about the aunt's intervention and only repeated their threats to the child for all to hear. In this way the child was made fully aware of the seriousness of his misbehaviour having indirectly received the harshest of sanctions, being kept away from his home, and this without direct punishment from his mother and without cause for bitterness.

While the social network of related women helped protect the mother from excesses in the direction of negative behaviour, the collective organization of the family and the harshness of daily life set a limit to the amount of care a mother could bestow on her child, thus eliminating the possibility of over-indulgence. The knowledge a mother derived from her personal intense observation of her own child, coupled with the information she gained by living closely with and observing other women and children, gave her sound criteria by which to mould her expectations of her children; she knew what tasks her child could perform unaided at any given age. Additionally, the harshness of living conditions and the hard labour demanded of every woman in order to secure the most elementary conditions for the functioning of the household, like water, heat, food, etc., pressured her to put this knowledge into practice with every child at all times. Thus the rural mother, while giving her children priority over everything else, would limit her caretaking to the level of the strictly necessary; that is, she would not dress a child who could dress himself, she would not feed a child past the age when he could do it alone.

The rural Greek mother did not have to submerge herself into the childhood culture to stimulate, to amuse, to occupy, or to instruct her children, replicating functions that others could fulfil just as well or even better at other times and other places. She just followed their development from the same stable stand point of the care-giver which no-one else could replicate. She established a pattern of interaction with each of her children where they would not turn to her over trivia, but only when her support was really necessary. This she would provide each and every time unquestioningly and unconditionally. In this way she gained in importance and stability, becoming the personification of support and care in its noblest form. Her continuous vigilance over her child during the first two years of his life and her ensuing effectiveness in anticipating needs and offering appropriate services without waiting to be pressured into giving them did set a pattern of give and take, which was based on appropriate offerings and not on demand. This pattern of offering before being asked gave the traditional rural mother the aura of unlimited generosity, while at the same time allowing her a benign control over the relationship. It would be no exaggeration I think to state that the image of the traditional Greek mother expanded to include the house, the home and the household, becoming the symbol of all that was personal, valuable and meaningful to the traditional person. The mother was not simply necessary to the house as Duboulay (1974) noted; she was the house, 'she embodied by her actions the physical as well as the symbolic aspect of the house and as such she represented in her own person' . . . 'the sanctuary from the hostility of both nature and society, a cornucopia . . . gained by family toil, the history and continuity of the family.' Like a solid tree I see the rural mother, fruit bearing and casting a cool shadow on a dry soil; source of life and strength; an indivisible part of the Greek land, poor yet hospitable. A tree that needs long years to grow and the protection of a group to blossom, with its roots firmly set in the tradition of centuries and its branches heliotropically orientated towards the cohesiveness of its social entourage.

PART II
THE ATHENIAN MILIEU

6 Social Networks: the Immediate Family Relatives, Friends and Neighbours

The city of Athens has changed so radically in the last twenty years* that when we speak of social structures of any kind we are in fact referring to processes in a state of flux. Not only has the number of inhabitants nearly doubled since 1961, but the qualitative changes have been staggering as well; especially so in the periphery of the city.

As mentioned in chapter one, the working class neighbourhoods I visited in 1968 bore a remote resemblance to the neighbourhoods I found when I returned in 1975–76.† New apartment blocks had replaced most of the old, somewhat dilapidated houses. The common yard shared by several house-holds, the nucleus of social interaction between several families, had disappeared and the street, invaded by cars, had lost much of its function as a place for children to play in and women to socialize. In the house interior, modern kitchens with flowery tiles and built-in cupboards had replaced the slummy kitchen–dining–sitting room of old.

Although in appearance the inhabitants of the new working class neigh-bourhoods bear all the characteristics of urban dwellers, the rural origin of the great majority of them is still reflected in many of the values they cherish. Despite the pronounced modification the traditional values have suffered in

---

* A brief resumé of the evolution of the Greek city and state during the last 150 years is presented in Appendix II.
† The information in this chapter is drawn from my personal contacts with working class mothers. These contacts took the form of systematic observation and interview-ing for the group of young mothers presented in chapter one or were mostly social in nature for numerous others I had worked with in previous research projects or just happened to know socially. Unless otherwise stated, the term Athenian in this chapter pertains only to blue collar workers and their families.

the urban setting, they have not yet been totally transformed. Foreign visitors staying in Athens for some time note that the anonymity of the large city has not yet eradicated the people-orientation of the traditional Greek. Lively social exchange has not disappeared altogether from the life of the working class family. Entertainment and celebrations of any kind, sorrows and calamities take on a strongly social character. On any special holiday— and the Greek Orthodox calendar has plenty of them—one can see Athenians lunching in restaurants, on the verandas of small country cottages, or picknicking by the seaside in large groups comprising several adults, children and some elderly persons. The working class family that would spend such days without friends or relatives is the exception rather than the rule.

This pronounced social predisposition still encountered in most Athenians is followed as well by a persistence in the traditional way of categorizing people as 'our own' and 'the others', with all the negative connotations associated with the traditional concept of 'the others' (i.e. the outgroup) and some of the positive qualities still attributed to the ingroup people. As for the numerous people belonging to the category of fellow citizens, with whom urban living brings one into daily contact, a cognitive-emotional construct of neutral gradation does not appear to have developed yet in the minds of most Athenians. Norms of civil conduct, i.e. polite and detached, befitting the reality of urban living being almost non-existent in Athens, living and working in this city can be hazardous to one's mental and physical health. The reason can be easily understood when one considers that for the average Athenian all his fellow citizens, from the anonymous other who happens to drive in front of him or shop in the same store to the co-worker who is not a declared friend, each one of the 3 000 000 Athenians is viewed as one of 'the others' whenever encountered and is treated accordingly, i.e. pushed, cheated, antagonized, superceded, etc. as befitting the situation.

In the last couple of years daily living in the city of Athens has become increasingly difficult. One of the reasons (and certainly not the only one) has been the transformation of the city into a megalopolis, which has not been followed by an equivalent change in the mentality of the people, politicians and citizens alike. To take driving as a simple example, as long as there were but a few cars on the streets undisciplined and antagonistic driving caused only few accidents; now that the number of cars has multiplied the number of casualties has reached alarming proportions.

Going back to the young mothers who concern us here, the group of women I observed represent the first generation of working class Greek women, who have had to cope with an urban way of life without all the social supports of the traditional rural culture that had survived until about 1960. For reasons mentioned in the historical survey (presented in Appendix II), in Greece more than in other European countries rural life is associated with poverty, backwardness and low social prestige. Urban migrants, who consti- tute the majority of the working class, simultaneously accept and negate their rural heritage. The young mothers I observed are mainly second generation urban migrants, raised in Athens by rural parents. The concur- rent juxtaposition of the traditional and the modern is personified by their parents on the one hand and their friends and neighbours on the other. To the extent that both are very much part of their lives, it is to be expected that the young mothers' values and living patterns would be a mixture of modern and traditional elements. As is usually the case, the more superficial aspects of their existence, like style of dress, manner of speech, smoking, drinking and getting personal with men, are greatly affected by modernization, while the more basic life values pertaining to family, religion and self-identity retain much of their traditional character.

Beyond the specific traditional elements present in the attitudes and behaviour of modern working class Athenians that give them their particular Greek character, Athenians of the seventies and eighties are exposed to certain social conditions which place them on the same footing as modern city dwellers the world over and very much apart from their rural ancestors. The main common factor found in large urban settings is, as I see it, the absence of stable social formations. The social groupings that develop have no continuity over time nor any stable identity over and above the individuals comprising them. Entities like the extended family, the neighbourhood and the community exist mostly in name, fulfilling none of the functions which they did in the rural milieu. Friends and relatives in the city can possibly play some of the roles the ingroup played in the village, but the extended family, like the village, was a stable whole which was more than the sum of its parts. It functioned like a supersystem for the individual members; it moulded their behaviour, up to a point, to make it fit the functioning of the whole and offered a frame and a context for all human exchanges. In contrast, urban nuclear families, like friendships, are just a sum of interpersonal relation- ships between the individuals comprising them. They reflect the strengths and weaknesses of the individual members, gaining in cohesiveness or heading to dissolution according to the members' interest in them or lack of it.

Only work affiliations have in the city the context, structure and functional subordination characterizing traditional social affiliations. But, whereas work relations in an urban setting usually only touch upon part of an individual's needs and activities and mostly on a temporary basis, the traditional extended family covered all aspects of life making for greater interdependence between the group members.

If in Athens today most working class people have around them a network of relatives and friends with whom they are in close contact, this is more out of individual choice rather than the result of a social reality that necessitates and facilitates such contacts. In other words, Athenians must, in order to sustain their human ties, initiate independently each and every contact, since the work, social and religious rituals that brought village people together daily have almost disappeared from the life of the average urban dweller.

Human relationships, important as they were in the traditional milieu, were not an aim in themselves. They were subordinated to the family ecosystem of which they were an integral part, and were moulded and sustained by this system, while in the city human relationships outside the nuclear family have mostly an autonomous function; they are peripheral to one's basic life pattern and can be continued or terminated by choice, with little consequence. The freedom of choice to have or not to have a network of relatives and friends around the immediate family is an important differentiating factor between a collective and an individualistic culture. The Athenian family of the eighties may choose almost invariably in favour of the extended family affiliations, bearing a seeming resemblance to the traditional rural family. However, the fact that Athenians meet out of choice or obligation, but not out of vital necessity, places them far apart from their rural ancestors as far as the quality of the interaction is concerned.

A. The urban family: from collective to interpersonal

In the Athens of the eighties, like in every other large urban centre, the family is a dynamic field of interpersonal relationships. Even when the individuals comprising it are bearers of a traditional culture with a traditional way of viewing it, within the given structure of the industrial–technological society, the family ceases to be a collective unit and is subtly transformed into a network of interpersonal relations. Outside the walls that mark its physical boundaries the family ceases to exist. Each person becomes an individual the moment he steps outside the confines of his house and, except for extreme cases of notoriety (either positive or negative) of one of its members, the family one comes from is non-existent beyond the level of the general socio-economic background it provides. At school, at work, in the shops and in the streets one is just an individual and is treated according to the way one appears and behaves. The individual does not usually carry with him the reputation of the family he comes from, either as a shield or a stigma. Within society at large he functions as an individual and as such he returns to his family in order to meet his personal needs. The absolute identification of one member with another, which bound the traditional rural family together, has broken down in Athens for lack of objective reasons to justify and sustain it. The sense of 'we-ness' emanating from this identification was replaced by a feeling of 'I and you' and the unconditional loyalty to the family has become, in the best of cases, a conditional attachment to parents and siblings.

In the mind of middle-aged people or older there may still exist notions and myths of collectivity. For young people, however, whose mental constructs are formed mostly on the basis of lived experiences, the family must, I presume, consist of just the sum total of their one to one relations with parents and siblings and little else; the sense of family being as strong as the overall feelings invested in these relations. In modern society, where the mode of production depends on individual performance, social niches are cut in terms of individuals and not in terms of families. Since the family does not constitute a considerable economic entity it has become a peripheral institution with specialized functions, and outside of these functions it is non-existent.

The use of the same word 'family' to designate the stable, tightly knit production unit found in the traditional rural milieu and the changeable, loosely articulated social institution encountered today in the modern city is quite misleading. The transformations which the family institution went through following the transition from a rural to an urban way of life are nothing short of the metamorphosis we would witness in a modern economic conglomerate, like IBM for example, if it were stripped of its functions as a full-time producer of computers and only periodically turned out a model or two, remaining in existence mostly for the social benefits its employees derived from their contact with each other. Far-fetched as this example may sound, it does give an idea of what has happened to the Greek family in the course of the last fifty years, whereupon an institution that was designed to meet people's each and every need (economic, social, educational, emotional, sexual and existential), had its functions curtailed mostly to a single short-term role (i.e. a reproductive one), losing in the process its social identity and its functional autonomy.

Athenians of rural origin who are now over forty years of age are the ones who lived through this transition most fully and have suffered from it the most. No matter what course of adjustment they may have chosen, the feeling of an experienced loss surfaces as soon as one takes the trouble to ask a few questions. Some tried to accept the movement of the times by allowing within their own family some inevitable changes, while resisting those they could. Others tried to deny the inevitability of change by scapegoating and attributing the responsibility for it to the communists, the hippies or the politicians. Still others acted as if they were all out for modernization and liberation from the bondage of the family. Whatever course each may have followed, and I am sure there are as many variations as there are Athenians, the one characteristic all of us born before the war have in common is our persistence in attributing to the family more importance than it has in essence. We refuse to accept that the investment made in the family by ourselves and our children should be equivalent to the function it fulfils, no more and no less.

It is hard to tell whether habit alone or a basic human need for belonging to a stable social unit compels us to go on treating the family as an institution with continuity across generations. The notion that the nuclear family—in contrast to the traditional extended family—falls into disuse as its offspring come of age is still almost unthinkable in Athens. As a result of an often unrealistic loading of the family institution, many of the normal evolutionary changes occurring in the life of growing children, and especially those signalling their passage into adulthood, tend to become for many Athenians sources of embarassment or major crises. For example, children's education or professional employment, mate selection, their place of residence after marriage and the names they will give their children are often associated with frustration and disappointment for parents. Across social classes, differences concerning parents' attitudes toward adult offspring are quite pronounced. Generally speaking, one could say that members of the middle classes, in contrast to blue collar workers and the economic or intellectual elite, are the ones who adhere more closely to the traditional model of the family. Not in essence of course, since this is no longer possible, but at least in the ritualistic aspects.

From the economic point of view, middle class parents seem to have more influence over their children and can control their behaviour the most. If we take for example the living arrangements of young middle class couples in the Exarchia* district, we see that the majority (60%) live with or very close to their parents (37% with the wife's parents and 23% with the husband's parents), either in homes which the women have received as a dowry upon their marriage or in houses owned by the husband's parents, which are large enough to accommodate two families. In working class families who cannot afford to own a house and the one they rent is not large enough for two families, newly married couples live alone as a rule and only take a parent to live with them when he or she is widowed and can no longer live alone. The majority of working class Athenian mothers I observed lived in rented apartments and were specifically selected as not having a living-in parent.

From what I understood, the choice of the district young couples settled in after marriage was arbitrary, up to a point, depending on the friend or

---

* A middle class Athenian neighbourhood surveyed by anthropologist Helen Zatz (1981).

relative who would happen to spot a suitable flat for rent in his own neighbourhood when the young couple were in need of one. Being close to the parents' house was not a consideration that seemed to play a determining role in the choice of an apartment. This was especially true at the time of marriage, at which time young people's feelings, the girl's in particular, towards their parents are often quite ambivalent. After the birth of the first child, grandparents on the mother's side appear to gain in importance and if convenient an effort is made to decrease the distance between the two households. The central issue accounting for most of the tension between parents and daughters in their teens and twenties is the amount of freedom girls can enjoy prior to their marriage, with parents still cherishing idealized notions about the importance of chastity and young girls playing it down.

Working class girls usually enter the labour force after they complete the nine years (six until 1976) of compulsory education, unless they do particularly well at school, in which case they continue with their education. They usually give most of the money they earn to the mothers who are in charge of the family budget. Unless something extraordinary happens to the family, the daughter's money is kept separately to be spent on the preparation of her trousseau. Families who cannot provide their daughters with at least a small flat as a dowry cannot aspire to an arranged marriage for them. In such cases—which actually form the rule for the working classes—parents tend to view their daughters' virtue as their greatest asset, while daughters rely mostly on their personal charm to attract a husband. Young working class girls who work outside the home and have a steady income, albeit quite modest, who must fend for themselves most of the day, who must form their own circle of friends from among their colleagues and rely on their own skills to find a suitable husband, can hardly be expected to show as much blind obedience to the parents and loyalty to the family as rural Greek girls did a couple of decades ago. But quite a few working class parents—most of them of rural origin—expect just that and feel personally humiliated when their daughters act independently.

Even for boys, who have traditionally enjoyed much greater freedom than girls, friendships and social involvements outside the family are often a source of tension with parents. As I see it, the great disequilibrium noted in many Athenian households with grown children is probably due to the fact that the social autonomy enjoyed by young people today tends to uncover the weakness of the family as an institution with stability and continuity. When adolescents begin to establish close relationships with people outside the family this instead of enriching the family weakens it, for young people are seen as spending outside the family circle the only ingredients that keep it together. To working youths what else can the family provide other than emotional support? Thus, turning to friends for advice and comfort can be viewed as withdrawal from the family; as a refusal on the part of the young ones to take from the family the only thing it can possibly offer.

In the traditional milieu, where children from their early years functioned as representatives of their family on all occasions, they did not usually have personal attachments. Wherever they went they were treated by adults and children alike on the basis of the existing relation between the families they respectively came from. In the rare instance where a child would happen to form a bond with a person from an unknown family, whether a friendship with a peer or a work relation with an adult, the bond would automatically serve to bring the two families together. As long as the bond continued the two families considered each other an ingroup.

As recently as the late fifties in Athens, when many a business was similar in scale and structure to the rural family enterprise, children reaching the age when they could begin to work were placed by their parents in the family business of a relative or a friend, the expectation being that the child's boss and his family would become an ingroup to the child's family. When a friend of mine living in the outskirts of Athens married off her daughter in 1969, three of the more expensive wedding presents were sent by a store and two workshop owners where her other children worked.

From the mid-sixties onwards, the city's accelerated development dissolved the microscale of the traditional Greek milieu. The neighbourhood ceased to function as such and the small family enterprises were gradually replaced by large impersonal firms. In the process, each person came across several people known to him only from school or work, who could not possibly become assimilated by his family on account of numbers and distance alone. It is then I believe that the traditional Greek family received the final blow, being transformed de facto into a modern institution, where the collective spirit was replaced by individual freedom and cohesiveness and continuity were replaced by fragmentation of functions and discontinuity across generations.

B. The relatives

The average Athenian young couple is surrounded by a number of relatives with whom they have a close relationship. They are usually the siblings and their spouses, or alone if single, and occasionally a cousin or two. The couple does not necessarily keep close contact with all the siblings on the man's and the woman's side. Usually one or two are chosen, from the one side or the other, that meet the general criteria of similarity and practical convenience; like similarity of age and economic status, plus proximity of living place.

Married brothers or brothers-in-law seldom do business together and if they happen to have common financial interests it is more often a source of tension and friction than a unifying factor. In the case of need they do lend money to each other with the clear understanding that it is to be returned as soon as possible.

Essentially, what they offer each other is human contact during leisure hours, Sundays, holidays and name days for example. Relatives meet regularly to eat together and share each other's troubles. They comment on important events, trying to make some sense out of the incoming information. Men discuss political and economic developments while women focus mostly on human affairs, marriages, divorces and the like. Usually relations among relatives are quite stable and the break when it occurs is, more often than not, due to conflict over economic matters, such as differential economic development or suspected lack of generosity. There is a common saying, illustrating the fact that business deals are not likely to be successful among relatives, 'Μέ τόν δικό σου φάε καί πιές καί κολιγιά μήν κάνεις', 'eat and drink with your kin but conduct no business together'. Sincerity in the interaction between relatives obviously depends on the individuals involved, but as a rule I would say that there is no effort made to show off or to appear better off than in reality. Financial difficulties are usually discussed quite openly and so are the children's misbehaviour and problems of all kinds.

Gatherings among close relatives on ordinary weekday evenings, when the number is small, are usually comfortable, relaxed and somewhat boring. On holidays, when the mood is festive and the number large, gatherings become vivacious and noisy, the spirits are high and the conversation (if it may be called that) incoherent with everybody talking and laughing almost at the same time. To a Northern American or a Western European observer the interaction among relatives in a typical Athenian family gathering would appear most intimate, but this closeness is a far cry from the identification found among the members of a traditional extended family. On the other hand, the bonds between relatives of the working classes appear to be considerably closer than the relationships among affluent Athenians. Upper middle class family gatherings can be quite formal and pretentious, with people interacting without much interest in each other beyond the level of mere curiosity expressed in often meaningless chat.

My observations have led me to think that intimacy in human relations is related to need, with the difference becoming apparent, not in terms of the number of people with whom one keeps some form of contact, but in terms of the quality of the interaction. Similarly, Athenian non-working mothers are often surrounded by quite a few women friends and neighbours, usually with same age children, whom they see quite frequently but with whom the relationship is mostly situational. The closeness will exist for as long as the geographical proximity exists, but will wane if they happen to change neighbourhoods. These neighbourly contacts between women, that usually begin with exchanges of small services and gradually progress to lengthy visits, may become family affairs with joined evening outings and Sunday excursions, including husbands and in-laws on both sides. Alongside, misunderstandings and hurt feelings become as much part of the picture as the exchange of services and confidences, and fluctuations between intimacy and hostility are a continuous part of the relationship, reflecting the dissimilarity of attitudes and interests on the one hand and the common need for contact on the other.

In the households I observed, the relationship between friends and neighbours appears to be secondary to that of relatives, despite the fact that neighbours may be seeing each other more often. When it comes to borrowing a considerable sum of money or seeking an important favour, most of the women said they would turn to a relative, commenting on the transient nature of friendship.

In concluding, I would say that working class Athenian women seek in the company of relatives and neighbours some security against unforeseen adversity, stimulation and entertainment during leisure hours and a loose social frame, that works as their point of reference within the anonymity of the city. In contrast, rural women view their relatives and ingroup as their lifelong associates in all of life's expressions. Affluent Athenians on the other hand depend on others for even less than working class people do; with human bonds in these three groups being shaped and cemented accordingly.

7   The Athenian Mothers

A. Role, status and identity

If I think of the young women I worked with in the Athens area, who were chosen in an attempt to draw a generalized profile of a group of working class mothers, I realize that the differences between them were as striking as the similarities. If for the purpose of this book I must make certain generalizations, this is done by eliminating many individual particularities, a lot more than were apparent in the rural group. The twenty women I observed systematically were chosen to be as much alike as possible. As mentioned in chapter one, among other characteristics they were chosen to have in common, they were all non-working, raised in Athens by parents of rural origin and they did not have a living-in parent. Yet, despite the similarities, many differences were noted among the Athenian women, from their manner of dress to the hospitality they showed towards me, or the arrangement of their homes and the amount of socializing with neighbours; a clear reflection of the pluralism of city life as opposed to the uniformity of the traditional rural milieu.

Most of the women had worked before their marriage, some stopped when they got married and some when their child was to be born. In all cases, however, it seemed the obvious thing to do and there was no difference of opinion between husband and wife on this matter. Some had adopted a more modern style than others, smoking, dyeing their hair and fingernails and wearing modish clothes on their outings. Yet, as far as their attitude towards the family was concerned, there appeared to be a striking consensus. Their self-perception was inseparable from that of mother and housewife, with every other activity seen as subservient to this role. As I see it, working class Athenian women work exclusively in order to help the family, just as their ancestors worked in the fields. They usually seem to 'carry' their home with them at work, investing in the job as little energy as absolutely necessary. Athenian employees, especially civil servants who receive the minimum of supervision and run no risk of dismissal, are seen calling home every now and then. They talk endlessly with their colleagues about home economics, exchanging recipes and bargain addresses, looking and acting annoyed when they must attend to their business. Those who can afford to stop working when they have a child will do so even if they may regret it a little bit. As a rule they do not seem to consider the possibility of staying on at the job and hiring someone else to look after their child; not unless they will be making a lot more money than they would be paying the hired caretaker.

Towards their husband they no longer assume a submissive attitude, neither in public nor in private, but they do assume all the traditional responsibilities of housekeeping and child care. While they have only one child and do not work outside the house, young mothers do not expect their husbands to help them with housework or child care. From what I had noted in 1970 in an observational study focusing on the role of grandmothers in infant development, young Athenian mothers did not even allow grandmothers who lived with them to help much in child care, especially with their first born. They willingly accepted help in housekeeping but kept for themselves the care of the child, asserting in this way their identity as mothers.

In comparison to the observations I made during the late seventies, I formed the impression that the relationships across generations are becoming progressively more complicated. Women tend to keep a closer relationship after marriage with their own parents than was traditionally the case, while the husband's parents are now kept at a much greater distance than was traditionally customary. In both cases, however, conflicts and resentments are as much a part of the picture as concern, care and intimacy.

Listening to many of the young mothers talk about their own mothers and seeing them interact with them, one forms the impression that two opposing forces are at work at one and the same time. On the one hand they appear to long for company and support; they call their mothers on the telephone almost daily, they invite them over, they go and visit them, they ask for services and often complain that their mothers do not respond readily enough to their needs. On the other hand they accuse them of spoiling their child and mingling in their personal affairs. While they seem to need and care for each other, young women and their mothers reveal in their interaction some kind of hidden antagonism. I believe that in Athens today this attitude is beginning to find its way into most family relations where it was traditionally non-existent, the main reason for it being social and not intrapsychic.

Modern consumer society offers many opportunities for variety in life styles and even emphasizes pluralism, novelty and uniqueness, making a value of differentiation. While in the past people tried as best as they could to assimilate the examples set by others, now we deliberately try to be different, asserting our identity through our own personal performance.

This tendency for innovation, which we are not always aware of, often reflects modern man's painful effort to come to grips with new life situations for which no satisfactory approach can be found from the stock of traditional experience. Far from being just a modish affectation, the need for innovation affects the most central life decisions as well as the more peripheral issues—like mode of dress. Women in their role as mothers and housewives are no exception to this trend and consequently, as they try to set up their home, prepare their meals and raise their children in their own way, they come into conflict with their parents and in-laws. The discussions and arguments between Athenian women reveal that differences of attitude and of basic assumptions are very much at the root of most conflicts.

In the traditional setting, when women gathered together on any particular occasion, their exchanges centred around possible strategies and courses of action which would lead to a desirable end. What was never discussed was the end itself, for the basic assumption about the desirable outcome was commonly shared by all, dictated by a common value system. Whether the discussion pertained to peripheral or to the most central of issues, the pattern appeared virtually the same. For example, rural women in discussing feeding would be exploring alternative ways of preparing and offering food that would make a child fat; similarly discussions of morality would consist of descriptions of various acts judged as virtuous or immoral. An ideological argument about the desirability of fatness in babies or virtue in women would be unheard of, since there was *a priori* agreement on these issues.

As I see it, when there is an agreement about the desirable outcome, differences of opinion centre on specifics of action and are enriching to the people involved, for they help to clarify all possible facets of the solutions at hand. However, when basic assumptions are questioned the exchange of ideas can often become meaningless. When two mothers discuss different approaches to making a baby fat they are enriching each other's repertoire of action, thus offering each other added flexibility in meeting environmental and/or individual variations. On the other hand, the arguments presented by one mother in favour of fatness in infancy are of little use to a mother who has opted for leanness. As long as there was a shared goal to a given task people could co-operate by peforming the task jointly or taking turns, with the one taking over where the other left off. But when the goals are divergent co-operation can very easily turn into a power struggle. As long as the differences exist co-operation can only be attained by one person subordinating their beliefs to those of the other. Theoretically, one could argue that, in the case of two opposing views, discussion could lead to a new synthesis acceptable to both parties. In practice, however, one seldom sees such a synthetic process, especially as an outcome of a discussion between people who are a generation apart. As a rule, elders present arguments in support of their views based on facts that existed in their time, while young people draw their evidence from their immediate reality. So the chasm remains and the co-operation, if attempted, is plagued by inherent contradictions.

When the more differentiated Athenian mother asks her own mother for help she is implicitly saying 'come and help me do things my way'. This demand places the older woman in a difficult situation for she is denied the opportunity to share her experience, which she considers her greatest asset, and is only asked to perform manual work which she has some difficulty in carrying out due to her age. As a result, the co-operation is seldom if ever as smooth and satisfactory as they would both hope for. The bitter truth may be that when one wants to do 'one's own thing' one can only do it alone. Individuality runs a course opposite to co-operation. This opposition is, I believe, an integral part of modern Greek society reflected in all forms of human relations. Loneliness we dislike and a close co-operation based on identification we can no longer attain.

In the domain of child-rearing, the movement away from traditional practices entails for the young mothers many more difficulties in addition to the alienation from the elders, for mothering cannot fit in very smoothly with the social imperative for change and innovation. As I see it, the mothering role is essentially a responsive one and is recognized as such by society at large. I can think of no mother, or father for that matter, who achieved notoriety in Greece or elsewhere by successfully applying her or his innovative talents on the child-rearing task. B. F. Skinner, who attempted to do so by developing a special crib for his baby daughter, received more criticism than praise, mostly for trying to introduce innovation regardless of the outcome of his 'experiment'.

Mothering is a role which calls for a certain amount of conservatism and other-directedness. This may be one of the reasons why, at a time when creativity equals fundamental innovation, child-rearing is not considered a very creative task (whereas in the traditional rural milieu creativity in art like in everyday living was achieved through original rearrangements of the given patterns).

In the final analysis, urban mothers appear to be caught in the middle of two opposing currents. The imperative to keep up with their time and live up to the stereotypes presented by the mass media compels young mothers to break away from many of the traditional practices of their mothers' time; even if this is alienating them from their elders and depriving them of the security of the known path, leaving them instead to struggle unaided along the bumpy road of trial and error. Yet, this trial and error does not even have the charm of exploration, tainted as it is by the anxiety of groping in the dark. Mothers are not expected to discover new ways of handling their children, but simply to decipher the often vague, cryptic and conflicting messages issued by the experts and to apply them to their own and the child's everyday reality; they are not trying to work out a new pattern, but simply to detect *the* correct one. Thus they can neither claim the status of an innovator nor can they enjoy the security of treading on the beaten track.

Not only do urban mothers enjoy a lower social status and have less self-assuredness in comparison to the traditional rural mothers, but the overall satisfaction which Athenian mothers can derive from their role is also more limited. By performing their mothering role rural women had, in most cases, a full share of all their world could offer; the ultimate social value was other-directedness and they were its personification. The scene where the most important and meaningful events took place was the home and they were its principal manager and living symbol. For the urban mother the goods displayed in the consumer society window are not within reach, the rewards provided for excellence are not for her kind; the home is just a preparation and recuperation station while the real life is lived 'out there'. Mothers are in the same footing as all workers in the service professions, enjoying a certain respectability without any claim to fame or power.

For Athenian working class women, the distance separating them from the models attracting the limelight is more the result of their social class than a consequence of their social role. Economic as well as cultural–educational factors exclude them from 'creative' employment and 'creative' leisure. In the dehumanized production system of our time there is no doubt that child-rearing, even under deprived conditions, is by far the most creative task a woman with limited education can perform. For this reason, probably, working class women still view mothering as an all-important role and seem to experience little difficulty giving up professional employment to devote themselves to their family. If, however, they do not question the decision they are bound to question the rewards. The echo from the past still lingers on and the resonance of the present life as lived 'out there' is made too loud by the mass media to be ignored. The comparisons, which are inevitably made, highlight the marginal aspect of a home-bound existence. In the average Athenian home, the social and emotional rewards, the interpersonal intimacy and social prestige enjoyed by rural women cannot be had today. However, neither can most of the material goods which in our consumer society are advertised for all to see but few can reach.

B. The husband–wife relationship

For the husband–wife relationship in Athens I know in fact less than I do for the rural couple, paradoxical as this may sound. For one thing there are considerably more studies made on the rural Greek family than on the urban one and for another I myself had fewer opportunities to systematically observe the urban husband–wife pair interacting. In the villages where we conducted the observations, men returned home for lunch around 12 o'clock noon while I was still there observing the child. On rainy days many of them did not go to work at all; they just went to the café, after having spent a good part of the morning at home playing with the child. Whether the husband returned early for lunch or was at home when I arrived, not having gone to work, I did not feel in the rural homes that my presence and the husband's were in any way mutually exclusive. In the Athenian homes, however, I clearly felt that I had to leave as soon as, and preferably before, the husband got back from work.

The differential nature of their work probably accounts to a large extent for the differential attitudes of rural and urban men towards a visitor. When rural men return from work they seek physical rest and social stimulation, for their jobs often entail much physical exertion but little if any psychological stress; while urban men seek mental relaxation above all on their return home, which the presence of a stranger does not facilitate. This mental fatigue experienced by the men of the urban households must have an influence on the husband–wife relationship as well. A man struggling in a city as disorganized and chaotic as the city of Athens and a woman secluded in the micro-world of the apartment block live in different worlds and are bound to have quite different needs.

From the discussions I had with the urban women, I formed the impression that their relationships with their husbands were not in most cases very close ones; anyway not as close as they would have liked them to be. Lack of care is what most women I talked to accused their husbands of, but this is also what men blamed their wives for. Whatever it is that men and women need of each other it does not seem that today in Athens we are quite able to get it. Are we asking too much of the relationship? Are there biological differences that prevent men and women from assuming interchangeable roles in caring for each other? Or is the life we lead responsible for draining our ability to offer human concern and care? The reasons must be numerous and hard to overcome, otherwise the longing for companionship is such in the urban milieu and so hard to satisfy outside the home basis that couples would be forming impartible units. Yet, contrary to expectations, the husband–wife relationship appeared to be weaker among the urban couples I observed than the rural ones. I choose the word weaker to imply the existence of mutual dissatisfaction and unfulfilled expectations.

Listening to Athenian women talk about their relationship with their husbands—in response to my questions—I realized that their first commitment was to their child, with the husband occupying second position. The mother–child relation was perceived as being the closer and most important of family relations, whereas in the rural milieu women gave first priority to the husband–wife relation, although they did perceive the mother–child bond as the most intimate one. I had expected that the dissolution of the extended family and the ingroup would lead to a strengthening of the husband–wife bond. What I fear is happening instead is that the alienation characterizing the urban way of life, instead of improving the quality of the husband–wife relationship, simply forges the tolerance for a minimally satisfying relationship. At first I attributed this observed distance between spouses to traditional values and role patterns still lingering on in the urban milieu. I gradually realized, however, that the intimacy that was lacking from rural pairs would soon develop among Athenians if it was at all possible for them to meet each other's needs. Of the many forces that operate within the urban setting complicating the contact between husbands and wives, the one factor I came to understand quite well from my rural–urban comparisons was the corroding influence the urban way of life exerts on people's sense of identity and, by extension, on their ability to be giving and caring.

From my first contact with the rural mothers what impressed me most—as I have already mentioned in part one—was the self-assuredness these women appeared to possess. Not only did I see this in the women I observed, but I also began to experience it myself as I shared part of their daily routine. The concern shown by other human beings for the work we do, and not only for the end result but for the simple daily and hourly performance, is surprisingly ego building. It is not the praises and honours, not even the knowledge that what we do will be of some use somewhere, that count, as much as the direct feedback received from the interested presence of others with whom we share the simple acts that make up the whole. Their concerned look, their change of pace to accommodate their performance to ours, a smile or a timely word make up the recognition we are in need of.

I have the impression that my second generation urban compatriots and my Anglo-Saxon readers will accuse me of being romantic and over-emphasizing the benefits of collaboration. I can almost hear the protests: who says we need continuous feedback for the work we do? Do we not, urban men and women alike, make do without it? Why depend on others to evaluate our performance? With self-sufficiency as an ideal, dependence on others to give us our feeling of worth can be synonymous with weakness. That is how I myself felt, at least until I went to work in the Greek villages and briefly experienced something different. After that, having identified the importance of appropriate feedback, I recognize its effects in myself and others. I recognize the feeling of satisfaction derived when others care to give us an appropriate sign acknowledging our existence and our actions and the emptiness that invades us when this feedback is denied us. The first time I realized how little of this feedback our urban life offers us was at a friendly gathering I went to one Saturday evening two hours after I had returned from Epirus. I met there the circle of friends I consider to be my closest and only that evening, with the impression of the interaction of rural people still fresh in my mind, did I realize how little we care to look at each other, to listen, nod, smile and observe. Much as I knew about urban alienation and all its manifestations, only that evening did I pair the casual disinterested behaviour of friends to the feeling it elicited in me. It was only then that I understood why ever so often work meetings or friendly contacts in the city result in a feeling of fatigue and uneasiness, while conversations with near strangers in villages have occasionally given me an unexpected feeling of comfort.

I have gradually become convinced that the need for recognition, when unfulfilled, mars much of our life and our relationships. Our feeling of self-worth, so closely related to our peace of mind, depends to a large degree on the acknowledgement we receive from others that what we do matters. This acknowledgement is more rewarding I believe when it comes in the form of immediate feedback to our everyday actions from the people we work alongside, than when it takes the form of public acclaim for our contribution as a whole. The rewards of any kind we may receive at the end of a year's conscientious work can hardly give us a lasting satisfaction that will counterbalance the daily impression of a life spent among competitive, hostile or simply indifferent co-workers. When the recognition comes for the finished product the pleasure I think is limited. In this case the relief and the sense of achievement we derive from the completion of the task far outweighs the satisfaction others can give us. When we come to weigh all the effort invested in a given endeavour against the rewards received for the end result I believe we invariably find the rewards lacking. 'For this I spent all that effort?' is the usual question that follows graduations, anniversaries, promotions and the like. This question usually surfaces shortly after the first excitement is over, bringing with it a feeling of emptiness and fatigue. If we can suppress the question, the feeling we can hardly escape. Ideally we ought to expect recognition from others only for the simple daily motions we perform, for which simple gestures of acknowledgement are sufficient recognition. For the end results we ought to expect nothing other than the inner feeling of satisfaction for a task completed. When, however, the prerequisites for the daily feedback do not exist, then we tend to reverse the order.

For the Athenian non-working mothers I observed and their blue collar husbands, the daily routine offers few opportunities for positive ego building feedback. Additionally, for these two groups in particular, the values of the consumer society do not allow them to believe that their overall contribution has any social prestige attached to it, despite the competitiveness and

7 The Athenian Mothers 89

indifference surrounding their job performance. For this reassurance which they miss in their daily routine they have to turn to their spouses, at the end of the day. Yet it appears that this mutual reassurance is not easily had, possibly because the long hours spent without intimate human contact leads people to adopt an uptight, uncommunicable attitude that is not easily reversible. Or it may well be that the differences in role performance make men and women ill equipped to really appreciate each other's daily tasks. Whatever the reasons, social and/or interpersonal, the fact remains that few people in Athens today feel that their efforts are being fully appreciated. Of all the married people I have known socially or professionally, I cannot think of a single man or woman who has not accused at sometime or other his or her spouse of being selfish and unappreciative. The difference between happily and unhappily married couples appears to be only a matter of degree in this respect.

The young mothers I observed and interviewed appeared to me, behind their resigned attitude, to nurture feelings of hurt and mild rancour towards their husband, which surfaced with the slightest provocation, without a clear awareness of what exactly they were expecting from him. In a way, they blamed him for the fact that his presence usually placed additional demands on them instead of alleviating the feeling of weariness accumulated during the day. As I understood it, women—and men as well—would have liked to find in their spouse a kind of colleague who would follow from afar and share emotionally their daily work in all its details; offering care and attention to remedy frustration and disappointments and sharing the satisfaction of minor achievements. This and only this constitutes valid proof that what you do matters to someone. When the husband—realistically enough—refuses to take seriously the child's misbehaviour that so upset his mother, or shows a total unwillingness to become involved in any housework, or fails to even notice the immaculate cleanliness of the house, he is in a way conveying the message to his wife that she spends her time and energy on matters of little importance to him. But if he does not care, who does?

I believe that in Athens today an unfulfilled desire for recognition is at the root of much of the dissatisfaction people express in relation to work and family relations. Closely entangled with all the specific claims that fuel strikes and divorces are complaints about lack of consideration. This may be a typically Athenian phenomenon, due to the fact that we are the immediate descendants of people whose culture was based on the value of 'honour', i.e. the good opinion of others. We may be urban misfits who have not yet fully adjusted to the transition that took place within the span of one or two generations, transforming the co-operation among closely identified relatives into the 'parallel play' among competing or indifferent strangers. Or it may be that the need for human feedback, reassuring us that what we do matters, is basic and pan-human, and while some people have learned to acknowledge it even when they cannot satisfy it, others have learned to suppress it like the Victorians did to sex. Whichever is true I do not know.

C. The community of women

I must state at the beginning that the heading of this section may be misleading, for calling the social gatherings of Athenian housewives 'a community' is a misnomer. I have used it for comparison's sake only, in order to facilitate recognition of corresponding social formations in the rural and urban settings despite differences in specifics.

As will have become apparent by now, life in the Greek metropolis is too strongly coloured by the individualism imposed by present day economic and technological realities to leave room for collectivity, even in the most marginal of activities. Athenian mothers, like the rural ones, have around them a number of women with whom they share part of everyday life. However, while in the case of the traditional rural mothers the group of women was a cohesive and stable unit, in the case of the Athenians the relationships among women are just interpersonal affairs often changeable and transient. These relationships are rather shallow, covering a small part of the women's life, and lack the stabilizing influence of a group to protect the people involved from unrealistic demands, antagonisms and extreme criticism. Friendships among non-working urban mothers are usually formed on a neighbourly basis. Similarities in age and status and particularly some similarity in the ages of their children draw women who live nearby together and they begin exchanging services and visits, lengthy telephone calls, recipes and gossip.

Contrary to the visits between relatives who live at some distance apart, neighbourly visits are quite frequent, occurring almost daily. The time young mothers spend in the company of other women is a time apart in the course of their daily routine. It is a kind of interlude, time off from household tasks, and is devoted to the satisfaction of their personal needs. Usually women visit one another by mid-morning to have coffee together. Although the children are around, women and children do not form one group together; on the contrary, every effort is made to keep the children apart, contented and busy with a toy or a cookie, so that the mothers can have a chance to talk, smoke and drink coffee with a minimum of distraction from the young ones.

Instead of performing their daily tasks in the presence of others, urban women narrate their routine to one another. They give long exposés of their difficulties, their frustrations and their problems to their friends, but they usually live them out alone. Mothers, for example, who had difficulties feeding their child would wait for the visitors to leave before embarking upon the feeding trial, on the assumption, as I heard them say it, that external distractions would only aggravate the problem. This is in marked contrast to what used to happen even in Athens some five years ago, where problem eaters were systematically being fed in the park, on the street, in the yard or in the neighbour's house.

This particular difference in the behaviour of rural and urban women appears to have emerged spontaneously as a natural consequence of the social reality. The fragmentation of the urban way of life into public and private domains, personal and interpersonal, work and leisure, has gradually penetrated the world of mothering, despite the fact that it does not always fit there very smoothly. Quite often the little time off mothers try to secure for themselves is not granted to them; if their child happens to be somewhat irritable or unwell, his demands for attention become incessant and the flow of adult conversation becomes hard to keep up. Yet the rural pattern of 'socializing' and 'working' at the same time does not seem feasible in the urban setting. The continuous non-verbal feedback rural women offer each other, while they are also doing whatever needs to be done, presupposes a level of intimacy and identification which cannot be had in Athens today. In the absence of a truly collaborative relationship, urban mothers must content themselves with whatever else is available. A brief exchange over coffee, even with some whining and occasional cries as background, is better than no company at all. I believe that adults have certain needs for social exchange which they can only meet in adult company; a child cannot very well be his mother's work companion. In fact the demand which the child places on his mother for care and attention appears to make her more in need of adult company. This is possibly because the socially responsive aspect of the mothering role brings to the forefront of the mother's awareness her own need for attention and feedback; just as working in a bakery or a candy store must be particularly frustrating for someone observing a diet, as the ongoing activity is a constant reminder of this unsatisfied need for food which for people in a different setting might go unnoticed.

8   Growing up in Athens

The fragmentation of urban life offers us few opportunities to observe other people's daily living except for those we deliberately choose to become involved with. This applies to personal as well as scientific observation and for this reason the only age group of Athenian children I can speak with some certainty about are the 15–17-month-olds I specifically set out to observe. My professional contact with the urban mothers and the time I spent in their households did not offer me many chances to observe at any length infants or older children; for these age groups my knowledge is so fragmented that I can hardly attempt to present a cohesive picture. Thus my account will focus mostly on the toddlers whom I have observed systematically.

The majority of children I observed lived in two or three room apartments in recently constructed apartment blocks on the periphery of the city of Athens. Most of their day was spent indoors, except for a regular outing with the mother in the middle of the morning for the daily shopping and an occasional outing in the afternoon or evening with both parents for entertainment. Children spent most of their waking time in the same room as their mother, playing by her side while she was performing her housework. A good deal of the time they were in the mother's presence they were actually interacting with her (a similar pattern to that observed among rural mother–child pairs).

At night most of the toddlers slept in their own room, a practice recommended by paediatricians and maternity hospital personnel as conducive to the child's physical health. As I understood from the discussions I had with the mothers, upon their return from hospital they tried to follow the practices spelled out for them by the nurses and/or paediatricians. They all tried to breast feed their babies and most did so for an average of about two months. None of the urban mothers swaddled their babies in contrast to the rural mothers, who did swaddle them disregarding the repeated advice of the visiting nurse and paediatrician who were militant against this practice. For the sake of convenience, most Athenian mothers kept their newly born infants in the same room as themselves at night, but with the clear intention of moving them to their own room as soon as they stopped calling for food during the night.

At the time of the observation the children's daily activities consisted of manipulating household objects and toys, satisfying physical needs (eating, drinking, etc.), going from place to place, as they had just mastered walking or were about to, interacting with mother and occasionally interacting with visitors. In most households toys were not placed in a position where they could be freely reached by the children; they were placed high up on a shelf or in a cupboard and were given out by the mother one at a time, whenever the child seemed bored or restless. The toys were rather crude and unimaginative offering little opportunity for exploration and manipulation; dolls, plastic cars, a ball and an occasional rubber animal were the toys most often encountered. As a result, children did not seem particularly interested in their toys, directing most of their exploratory activity onto household items. On the basis of quantity alone object manipulation was clearly the central component of the child's daily activity. The child interacted with his mother much of the time he spent manipulating toys or objects, but he also spent time exclusively in object manipulation, significantly more so than rural children who were hardly ever seen involved in solitary object manipulation.

Although in terms of material possessions urban households were by far superior to the rural ones, in terms of the stimulation they could provide to a growing child they were rather poor. Both the number of people interacting daily with the child was more limited in the Athenian households and the environmental stimuli available in a small flat were minimal compared with the variety which the natural environment surrounding the rural houses provided. When toys and household utensils failed to satisfy the child's exploratory drive during the long morning hours which mothers and children spent at home and restlessness set in, mothers were often seen to pick up their child and to hold him up by the window to watch the street traffic as a diversion. Walking around the streets of Athens and looking up at the many windows and narrow balconies facing the street one can often see such a sight; a sight which predictably enough I never saw in the villages. In the rural households, when a mother or grandmother chose to direct the child's attention to a scene outside the house, she would invariably open the window (unless the weather was particularly cold), lean outside with the baby in her arms and talk to the people or even the animals on the street. The urban image I have in my mind, of the inactive mother–child pair staring with boredom and indifference out into the street, is a sad reminder of the confinement of modern Athenians within their own enclosed space; the sharp dividing line between private and public domains and the ever present threat of solitude this division entails.

For children as well as adults the lack of opportunities for brief and easy personal contacts, beginning and ending unceremoniously and repeated at will in the course of a single day, has far reaching repercussions. The choice we are usually faced with in the urban milieu is either to remain confined within our own house or to become involved in a somewhat prolonged and demanding interaction. Grandparents, aunts, uncles, friends and distant neighbours must, in order to interact with a child they are fond of, pay a pre-arranged visit that usually entails telephone arrangements, public transport, gift taking and discontinuity of the daily routine for all parties involved.

Most mothers complained that grandparents, and grandmothers in particular, spoiled their children and as proof of their claims they cited the fact that children became irritable and difficult to handle after the grandmother's visit. When I pressured them to tell me what exactly grandmothers did, which in their opinion was 'spoiling' the child, they gave me some minor illustrations that did not sound very convincing. They told me, for example, that grandmama gave the child candy when he should not be eating it or that she invariably tried to satisfy all his whims ('τοῦ κάνει ὅλα τά χατήρια'). However, I cannot easily accept candy eating or satisfaction of demands as causes for irritability, particularly when in the rural households I saw not one but ten different people respond alternatively to the child's demands, without him showing any sign of being spoiled or irritable. What I believe instead is that it is the nature of the visit *per se* which is at the root of the reported unrest. The long duration of the visits and their irregular occurrence account for a good part of the interpersonal tension caused.

The distance, social and geographical, separating most young parents from the grandparents tends to create a gap between them, which the grandparents attempt to bridge at every visit. Differential interests and occupations and the difficulty of sharing all the little daily satisfactions and annoyances tends to weaken the feeling of closeness between people, who often react by trying to cram all the missed exchanges into a single encounter. This results in a prolonged and loaded interaction which can eventually become very tiring. My contact with rural people has led me to believe that repeated brief encounters, embedded in the course of daily events, are usually a lot more lively, cordial and satisfactory than prolonged visits. This is unless of course there are special facilitating factors at work like sexual attraction, a common concern, etc. In the context of the urban way of life, I have noticed, among my own group of friends and relatives at least, that in a pre-arranged get together, where people interact for interaction's sake, communication tends to follow one of two extremes; it either tends to become superficial or quite intense and tiring.

I may be exaggerating in my admiration of the rural people's social performance, but, seeing the continuous on and off sequence of interactive events both among adults and between children and adults and the general climate of ease and calm in which the interactions took place, I am led to believe that this pattern is better suited to our needs than the one we urban dwellers are forced to adopt. The social pattern of urban dwellers entails long periods of time during which human exchanges are impersonal or non-existent, interspaced by infrequent but prolonged socializing intervals where some intimacy is sought. On the basis of this rationale, I suggest that Athenian children are, from a very tender age, exposed to the kind of human interaction which, although more agreeable than solitude, is often made by factors of reality to be overtaxing and not altogether satisfactory. The seeds of the ambivalence we adults often experience towards the people we call our own (friends and relatives) are thus sown from a very early age. The irritability which young children manifest as a result of their contact with grandparents is, I believe, the first manifestation of this ambivalence.

With the exception of their mother, the majority of Athenian toddlers who do not have a living-in grandparent do not seem to have a human presence around them on a regular basis. The only other person who has daily contact with the child is the father, but far too many changes in attitudes and work conditions must take place before Athenian couples begin to share even partly the tasks of child care. From the mothers' reports the father–child relationship appears to be somewhat peripheral and not altogether free of tensions and difficulties, consisting mostly of brief playing periods once or twice a day. In a statement that I found typical of most, one mother told me about her husband, 'he is very fond of his son and the baby reciprocates the affection, but he tires easily. He cannot stay alone with the child for long, he does not know what to do with him.' It is obvious to me that the same reasons that complicate the relationships of grandparents, friends and even of the mother with the child complicate the fathers' as well. If in the rural households mothers did not complain of their husbands' inability to handle their children, this was most likely due to the fact that men were seldom, if ever, given the opportunity to test the limits of their skills in this domain; father–child play always took place in the presence of several other men and women who were taking turns in interacting with the young child for very brief periods of time.

The way things stand today, Athenian toddlers raised by non-working mothers, who spend as much time interacting with them as rural ones and are surrounded by a network of grandparents, aunts and uncles who come visiting them regularly (about once or twice a week), are markedly less sociable than rural children. They are found to be less mobile in comparison (spending less time going from place to place), more object oriented (they spend more time manipulating toys and objects), more verbal, more demanding of their mothers (going after her, calling her, holding on to her), less responsive to her instructions and less sociable (they spend less time interacting with people other than mother).

This means that Athenian women, almost irrespectively of their values, their efforts and their future expectations, are raising children whose experiences and behaviour patterns differ significantly from those of rural children. The difference centres mainly on a dimension that is likely to play, with time, a determining role on the mother–child relationship. The main difference noted in the behaviour of rural and urban children pertains to the proportion of independent experiences in relation to social interactive ones and to responding versus demanding. What is remarkable, however, is that these differences in the social behaviour of rural and urban children become apparent from a very early age, before socializing agents outside the family, like school peers and the mass media, have come into play.

9   The Mother–Child Pair

My observations of the Athenian mothers interacting with their first born children convinced me of two things; first that difficulties in mother–child relations are an integral part of the urban way of life and second that solutions to problems in this area are neither permanent nor can they be attained by individual efforts alone. The best one can hope for with continuous effort is to cope and to learn to live with personal conflicts, but not to remove the causes or to resolve the problems; for I do not believe that there are individual solutions to social problems.

The urban mothers I chose to observe were selected, as mentioned in chapter one, to be as healthy and well functioning as possible, with special care taken to include in the sample women whose social and health history was free of complications. Additionally, due to their rural Greek heritage—which for all of them was only one generation behind them—these women shared a set of values that placed the utmost importance on the mothering role, calling for a total commitment to their children. Contrary to the trends of the time, the Athenian women I observed continued to invest a lot in love and interdependence. Instead of living their lives by the maxim 'I have only one life to live', they acted as if they were going to live their offsprings' lives as well; they thought of future happiness in terms of their children's welfare. This commitment on the part of healthy and able women on the one hand and their inability to establish a relationship with their children that would be consistent with this commitment on the other was to me the most telling illustration that human relations cannot be moulded at will in isolation from the social context.

When people fail or refuse to make an interpersonal commitment, we tend to think of this as being responsible for the failure or poverty of the relationship, but when the commitment exists we see that it alone cannot guarantee success. Recently, from the more developed countries of the West and the USA in particular, we have been hearing about the detrimental effects of the cult of narcissism. Even in Greece, we are beginning to feel that the number of people who live for themselves has been increasing of late.

Stories indicating that human relations are becoming brittle and precarious are proliferating. When confronted with the problem, many social critics (and most of us Greeks relish in this role) call upon a change of attitude as a first remedy; 'If only people—parents, children, husbands, wives—did not think of themselves so much, things might be different.' They react as if this withdrawal from the interpersonal to the individualistic sphere is the cause of all social evils, and not a mere defence reaction brought about by the very social conditions it is being blamed for.

Taking a close-up view of a small segment from the spectrum of human relations, the mother–infant interaction, I have become convinced that human relations at any given place and time evolve within limits clearly delineated by the existing socio-economic system. Individuals can improve or wreck their personal relations by their attitudes and behaviour patterns, but the optimum they can possibly attain is culturally determined. I have been led to adopt the view that the point where modern Greek culture draws the upper limit for possible satisfaction in human relations in general and the mother–child one in particular is low indeed, much lower than was tradition-ally the case, near threshold level most of the time, where satisfaction is so little it is barely perceptible.

In their daily interaction with their children, the Athenian mothers I observed did all that could be expected of a caring mother, and apparently a lot more than American mothers do for their children of the same age, in quantitative terms at least. By all appearances these mothers seemed to have established a very close and smooth relationship with their children. Only in comparison with the rural mothers could one note certain qualitative differences in the interaction which heralded possible long term difficulties; especially since urban mothers aspired to the kind of close relationship with their children that rural mothers enjoyed.

Thinking back to the mothers I observed, the first word that comes to mind is 'effort'. Again in comparison with the rural women, Athenians gave the impression that their daily interaction with their child was not something that came absolutely naturally, but was rather something that required special effort on their part. It was as if housework was their main task, while the demands of the child for attention were something which was calling them away from their 'work'. Although in theory mothers said that they gave their child priority over everything else, their husbands included, in practice they often behaved as if work was more important, albeit temporarily. Not that they ever refused, in my presence at least, to respond to any of the demands placed upon them by their child; it was mostly the determination with which they were carrying on their housework along or intermittently with child care that gave me this impression. Despite the fact that urban mothers had many more facilities than rural women they were more busy with housework during the morning and while supervising their child at play. Seldom did I see an Athenian woman just stand for any length of time observing her child like rural mothers did most of the day. Whenever, for example, they saw the child involved in a task that might at some point become mildly dangerous, eventually necessitating their intervention, instead of just standing by him to help when necessary, they would try to turn him away to something altogether secure.

This subtle difference in orientation between rural and urban women, which I would call a 'task-' versus 'people-orientation', seemed to appear in the Athenian working class scene after 1970. During the late sixties, when I conducted my first observational study of mother–child interaction, I visited more than sixty working class households and one of the things that did surprise me at the time, to the point where I still remember it 13 years later, was the clear hierarchy of priorities these women seemed to have, both in theory and in practice. Some of the houses I visited on some of the mornings when I entered for a pre-arranged visit were in a 'state of siege', dirty dishes in the sink, clothes all over the place, diapers put out to dry over and around the radiators (disposables were not widely used at the time), signs of the last meal still visible on the dining table and so on. The mothers would guide me through the mess with a casual comment 'with a baby around you know not much time is left for the house' and then they would go on unperturbed spending the greatest part of the morning interacting with the child. Only while he was napping did they try to perform the minimum necessary of housework. When aunts or grandmothers came in to help they were assigned some of the housework left behind but rarely were they asked to look after the child for any considerable length of time in order for the mother to gain some time off from child care. To them the child had first priority over everything and everybody else and there appeared to be nothing in their lives to draw them away from him.

In 1975 the interaction between mothers and their infants appeared to have lost some of its clarity. In the empty space of the three-room apartment some undefinable phantoms seemed to have cropped up attracting part of the mother's attention. Loneliness, value conflicts, doubts, insecurities, vague longings, whatever it may be it was energy absorbing, making it harder for the mothers to focus on the child and respond to his needs. The urban mothers' pattern of interaction with their children had, in relation to the rural ones', two important differences. The first notable difference pertained to the spacing of the non-interaction intervals. Urban mothers spent longer periods of non-interaction followed by equally longer periods of more intense interaction. While in the final analysis both urban and rural children had the same amount of interaction time with mother, for the ones exposed to the short intervals one could say that they had fewer experiences of separation and solitude. One needs to try and visualize the interaction in order to understand what this difference really amounts to. When the mother, while in the same room with the child, looked at him for a moment then looked away, touched him, gave him a helping hand then attended to something else, then looked again and looked away, the impression conveyed to the child, as I sensed it, was that the mother was continuously present for him. While in the case where the mother focused on some housework for ten minutes, then turned to the child for ten minutes, then to the task for 15 minutes and back to the child for 15 minutes more, the feeling created was one of separation and reunion alternating in time. It is quite likely that this pattern of separation and reunion is in a way related to the more demanding behaviour of the urban children, for they were seen—as mentioned in the previous chapter—calling the mother, going after her and holding on to her more often than rural children did.

The second significant difference in maternal behaviour was in the frequency of talking and looking behaviour. The single most frequent behaviour of the Athenian mothers was 'talking', and this often without looking at the child, for they talked twice as often as they looked at him. This decreased observation and increased verbalization as we move from the rural to the urban setting is I believe an important differentiating factor, flavouring the entire nature of the interaction. Much as I try to avoid simple one-way causative associations between maternal and infant behaviour, I cannot wave the impression of a close relationship between attentive observation on the mother's part and responsiveness on the child's part. It seems reasonable to assume that the more aware a mother is of her child's reality the more effective will her orders and instructions be. If the rural children's greater responsiveness to maternal instructions is to be related to one particular maternal behaviour I would say that the pronounced 'looking' which rural mothers do must be the one.

The question most puzzling to me, however, is why do urban mothers appear to be losing this particular skill for observation. In most respects they seem to act towards their children in the way traditional women did; responding to their child's every distress signal, showing a minimum of punitive, restrictive or reprimanding behaviour, responding to his social signals, fondling and caressing him moderately and often encouraging him to repeat an action he was already performing (a behaviour pattern analysed in some detail in Chapter 5), all in the same pattern as rural mothers. While in all the behaviours that entail activity and some exertion on their part urban mothers act like the rural women, in the most effortless one they lag behind.

Apparently, while the urban way of life did not change their basic values, for they are devoted to their children and try their best, it deprived them of a very basic skill; a skill that does not depend only on the repetition of a simple behaviour, but reflects also the general state the person is in. For I believe that only a person in a very peaceful frame of mind (or one who has learned to suppress all emotions) can stand motionless for any length of time and observe contentedly. The doubts, insecurities and occasional pangs of guilt which are part of the urban mothers' daily living are hardly conducive to the total other directedness which intense observation entails. In the final analysis, it appears that urban and rural infants are exposed to very different social realities, despite the seeming similarities in maternal behaviour.

As I see it, the presence of a cohesive social group not only affects the children directly, but indirectly too, through the influence it exerts on the emotional state of the mother. A woman struggling alone in an urban flat can in no way achieve the same results, on the socializing level, as the one who is part of a collective. It is the tragic fate of modern day Athenian women to want to preserve the traditional nature of the mother–child relationship and yet be unable to do so no matter how hard they try. The traditional closeness between mother and child from birth to death rested on the pronounced social orientation of the rural culture and the specific social skills that collective living reinforced continuously in mother and child. In the urban setting neither the social orientation nor the specific social skills are being reinforced in any way and so the relationship suffers. As I see it, the urban mothers' over preoccupation with house cleaning, their rather abrupt pattern of transition from child care to housework, their pronounced verbosity and limited observation—all the behavioural characteristics that differentiate the performance of urban from rural mothers—are the result of a different emotional state, and not of different beliefs, attitudes or intentions; an emotional state that is an inseparable part of solitary striving.

Athenian mothers, like their rural ancestors, are striving to do the best they can for their child. But 'the best' a somewhat frustrated and lonesome woman can do differs considerably from what a self-assured and contented woman can do. I believe that the main factor undermining the urban woman's self-esteem, making the task of child rearing so difficult in the urban setting, is the fact that every woman must struggle alone trying to discover at any given moment the behaviour that meets best her own needs and her child's. Over and above the detrimental effects that the lack of social prestige has on an urban mother's morale, the loneliness of the urban flat and the continuous reminders of 'life out there' from which she is cut off, what complicates her existence the most is the self-doubt she experiences due to a lack of consensus about her everyday acts.

The urban mother is left, more often than not, to her own hesitant ways to cope with the needs of her child; for her the only way to discover what should be done in response to a minor crisis is through trial and error. This way of learning is immensely taxing to the individual, especially when after an error there is no familiar correct behaviour to fall back on and, additionally, when there is no sure criterion of a correct response. Did the child fall asleep after prolonged crying because the last of several anxious attempts on the part of the mother to quiet him was the successful one, or did he just fall asleep out of sheer exhaustion? The only alternative to the trial and error approach is for the Athenian mother to rely on the information obtained from her mother and the next door neighbour (orally) or from the child care manual; information which in each case she would have to adjust to her specific reality. Whereas in the rural milieu the observation of other people's children is a comfortable learning experience, for the urban mother intense observation of her own child (which is all she has to observe) is a call for more differentiated behaviour on her part which she can hardly meet.

For the rural mother the notion of faulty maternal behaviour was non-existent. Well established traditions dictated her basic behaviour pattern and group living monitored her specific moves. The idealized Mother concept (with capital M) rested on infallibility and this infallibility was secured by the continuous and consistent feedback provided by other women.

The moment the element of error becomes an unavoidable part of maternal behaviour the attitude changes it brings along are far reaching. A very great sense of responsibility on the one hand and feelings of guilt on the other become part of the maternal predicament. Several urban mothers, when asked whom they would blame if an adolescent or young adult they knew broke away completely from his parents, said they would blame the parents. It seems to me that for parents to shoulder all the responsibility for the kind of relationship they have with their grown children is a somewhat exaggerated and unrealistic attitude to burden themselves with. For even if we opt for complete determinism we must still take into consideration the socializing influences outside the home, whose importance in modern cities we cannot underestimate. Rural women were much less inclined to consider parents as solely responsible for the behaviour of their offspring, despite the fact that in their milieu there were few if any environmental factors which might contribute to alienation of the young from their parents. I believe that this exaggerated sense of responsibility makes the urban mother feel as if she is under trial, waiting for the 'final judgement', a state of mind that can only cause anxiety in the mother and burden her relationship with her child.

In a day and age when the social forces at work tend to push people apart and when young people find the thread of communication with their elders cut off for various reasons (cultural, educational, social economic, occupational, etc.), I cannot understand how some young Athenian mothers can go on believing that their behaviour and that alone will be the only factor determining the outcome of their relationship with their offspring when the latter come of age. More than anything else, the unrealistic weight they attach to their own behaviour must in itself be an added reason for mothers to dread possible errors in their handling of their offspring.

If during infancy and early childhood the question of deciding what is right and what is wrong for one's child is often a difficult one to answer, as children grow up decisions often become impossible to make with any certainty. During the early years the child's physiological needs mark for the mother a rather clear course of action, but as development progresses complexity increases and choices multiply. Without a clear set of values, without models, appropriate training or direct feedback, urban mothers are groping in the dark for behavioural solutions that will be consistent with their inherited values, the demands of present day society, the advice of experts, their own needs and wishes, their child's, their husband's and possibly those of a couple of grandparents as well. This seems to me a most difficult predicament for anyone to be in. I can well understand why some women feel at a loss *vis-à-vis* their children and withdraw to a state of minimal involvement, while others adopt a pattern of ceaseless and often useless activity, while still others fluctuate between the two.

On the basis of the information I have gathered by living and working in Athens and by extrapolating from the research evidence obtained from the mother–infant pairs I observed, I would say that for the majority of non-working Athenian mothers the most typical pattern is the one entailing over-involvement from early childhood and all the way through adolescence. It is my impression that Athenian mothers tend to offer their services to their children not asking themselves how necessary they are to the children's well being, but rather as if they were trying to gain personal credit. They often appear as if they are struggling to get an 'A' for effort, or worse still, love for effort.

As children grow the role of the urban mother appears to change quite markedly. Peers and (sometimes) teachers begin to play an important role in the child's life and the mother's importance tends to diminish slowly, yet surely. As the child's life involvement increases the importance of the 'home' decreases proportionately, until it becomes like a relay station for him, a place for preparation and recuperation from the 'real life' experiences which are lived in the outside world. This transition is gradual for some children and abrupt for others, depending on the particular family, with the wealthier parents finding it easier to postpone the transition.

In the traditional rural settings, where the home remained the stable point of reference for adults and children alike, the mother kept her central position in the life of her children, despite the many changes that develop-ment brought to the specifics of the interaction. Past the age of four rural children clearly did more for the mother than she did for them in terms of errands and services. Yet her role remained all important as the giver of essentials for the children's physical and emotional well being.

In Athens today mothers are often seen performing tasks for their offspring which the children could well perform alone. A Sunday morning visit to some of the Athenian parks or squares is certain to provide an attentive observer with quite a few illustrations of mothers babying their school age children; tying their shoes, wiping their faces, putting on or taking off their sweaters etc. Yet, from the children's reactions, it would seem that the mothers do not gain their children's love and respect for the care they bestow. Even those mothers who do not feed, bath or dress their children past the age when they can do these things alone, only too often find themselves running errands for their children and spending time and energy on trivia. I have not followed step by step the process that leads to the mothers being ordered about by their children but I have seen this happen often enough to suppose that it has become common practice in Athens today. It appears that the traditional model of the all giving mother, when applied out of context, leads the mother into doing for the child many things he could very well do on his own, losing in the process much of her status and importance and becoming more of an attendant than a care-giver.

When in the home there are no animals or plants to be attended to, no work to be done in the fields, no herbs or wood to be collected from the mountains, water to be carried from the well or clothes to be washed by the river—all those tasks that were awaiting the young rural mother, even if pregnant, after her child completed his second year of life—what good reason can prevent an urban mother from doing for her child all she can to make life easier for him? When the choice is hers and hers only and the criteria uncertain, it is very hard indeed for the mother to decide what is good for her child and even harder to draw the line between unresponsiveness and over-indulgence. In the rural milieu not only did life's demands leave no room for over-indulgence, but also the live example of the others around them monitored the behaviour of both mother and child, to the point where rural mothers did not volunteer unnecessary services and children did not ask for them.

As I recall the many images of Athenian mothers walking their ten or even twelve-year-old children to school, in order to carry their bag when it gets too heavy, or running after them to bring them the sandwiches or the notebook that they left at home, or going to meet them from shool with an umbrella at the faintest suspicion of rain, I think in alarm that the line dividing caring from spoiling is a very thin one indeed. In fact it is a distinction which I believe a woman alone can hardly ever make with certainty. How can a mother with time and energy to spare be convincing in her caring image if she lets her child get wet, tired, frustrated in her presence without intervening to minimize the discomfort, either voluntarily or in response to his demands? How can she be sure of her own motives when she opts for the effortless alternative? If she decides to stay in the warmth of her flat instead of going out to meet her child in the rain, how can she be sure she is not acting out of boredom? On the other hand, a mother acting on her child's behalf every time he is in difficulty may well be depriving him of the opportunity to develop tolerance to frustration and problem-solving skills. If, however, she just ignores his signals of distress, letting him learn by doing, she may well appear in her child's eyes, and her own as well, as unresponding and uncaring. The problem is made more difficult as, in the seclusion of the urban flat, she has no way of really knowing how much stress a child his age can tolerate or what skills he can be expected to perform unaided.

'Independence training', which within cultures with long urban tradition is common practice, has not yet become part of the maternal repertoire in Athens (in the Greek language we have not as yet developed an equivalent term). This is most probably because our culture is still in transition and has not yet resolved the conflict.

In the traditional rural setting there was no need for the mother to train her children to be independent. This they learned by joining the labour force from a very tender age. Practical skills and problem solving abilities were acquired through collective living. Life in the common room and their participation in all life events, from quarrels to celebrations, to deaths, births and illnesses, taught the children all there was to know. Mothers just offered advice and support after the fact, helping children draw the 'right' conclusion, they never provided actual training. The small amount of time school age children, and boys in particular, spent in the mother's presence they could spend in being directly or indirectly nurtured by her without any risk of getting spoiled.

Urban children, on the other hand, can be quite shelterd from the realities of life. Unless the mother makes a conscious effort to delegate some responsibilities to them, refraining from helping them out, they run the risk of growing up dangerously naive and irresponsible. This additional require-ment of the urban mother may place yet another strain on the mother–child relationship. When it is the mother and not life itself that burdens the child with duties and responsibilities, which are mostly imposed for training's sake and are not really essential to anybody's well being, the child is bound to perceive the mother as an agent of oppression, even if only moderately so. Thus long term gains on the child's character are often achieved at some cost to the daily pleasures of the mother–child interaction. However, even the opposite course of action, that of continuous servicing, which Athenian mothers appear to be favouring does not guarantee a conflict-free relationship. When the mother adopts an attitude of pronounced involvement in the child's activities her interventions are often resented, even if some of the time it is the child who asks for them. Quite often the mother's involvement in the child's every move, in the way he dresses, eats, washes and studies, apart from the feelings of inadequacy it is bound to create in the child, also leads to a certain antagonism. The intervention is often perceived as a kind of pressure on the part of the mother to impose her way of doing things. Several times I happened to see Athenian mothers or even grandmothers bend in two in order to tie the shoelaces of a 10-year-old child, or to try to feel his socks to see if they were wet. The child's unco-operative reaction invariably made the sight a disagreeable one to watch. The one time I witnessed a similar scene in a rural household, the impression it created was one of great tenderness.

When the rural mother decided to attend to the needs of a grown child, she did this after conducting a skillful scrutiny of the whole household, something she did before every move. This informed her that this particular child was at that particular moment more in need of her attention than all the other people present and all the tasks at hand; either because he was hurt, exhausted, hungry, or cold. She would then perform her care-giving act, simple as it might be (such as taking off a pair of wet shoes), with all the seriousness and attentiveness we put into an act we know fulfills an important function. This attitude of gravity was conveyed to the other children present who, instead of resenting the fact that their brother or sister was monopolizing the mother's attention, tried to be of help—as children almost always do when they sense serious need—either by keeping very quiet or actively participating in fetching whatever was needed. Thus, in this type of interaction, the child found himself the centre of much care and attention when he needed it most, receiving in the shortest time possible the maximum of nurturance. The mother placed herself in a position where she could offer the most support with the least physical effort. This is the exact opposite to what the urban mother does most of the time; not out of choice, but in her effort to counteract the disruptive influences of our individualistic society.

When the family plays no role in modern society as an economic or social unit and is only called upon to offer its members the emotional support that will enable them to function best as individuals, when there is no common task to bring the family members together as a group, nothing important to carry out together, to plan, to share, to negotiate, the optimum vision of family cohesiveness we can realistically nurture is one where the individual members are trying with some success to share each other's disparate realities. In this fragmented context, what frame broader than herself, her values, weaknesses and personal ambitions, can the mother use as a compass for her actions? When the only bond connecting the members of her family, with their varied interests, occupations, problems and frustrations, is interpersonal attraction—the most fragile of all connecting fabric—how else can she hope to keep these bonds but through a maximum of offering, albeit uneccessary? After all, when there is no give and take what other signs are there left of family cohesiveness? As the traditional family group gave way to the sum of individuals we now call a family, the mother lost her traditional position as manager of the most sacred of institutions to become an attendant to the needs of each separate member of her family. Additionally, the modern way of life reinforced certain skills and attitudes that lead people, including mothers, into acting with no regard to relevance.

Rural women who lived in an orderly, hierarchically structured world had learned to view their children as part of the family whole, their immediate family as part of the extended family and so on; they had acquired a way of thinking and acting that entailed continuous comparisons relating the part to the whole. This gave them a sense of measure and appropriateness. Urban dwellers, exposed to an abundance of disjointed stimuli, are led to adopt an attitude of specialization, trying to focus on one thing at a time (i.e. housework at one time, child care at a different time), shutting off everything else and making each specific task an end in itelf (i.e. house cleaning for cleanliness' sake). In this context mothers lose much of their effectiveness and rewards become disproportionately poor.

The Athenian mothers I observed and interviewed seemed to be well aware that there was not much in store for them in terms of social or emotional rewards. In return for the effort they put into raising their children, all urban mothers said they hoped for was a minimum of recognition from their children when they were grown (νά μέ ὑπολογίζουν). They did not expect to be taken care of in their old age nor did they expect any material support. Their hope was to be allowed to see in their children the continuity of their own life; to see their adult offspring value what they stood for.

Unfortunately, pluralism and the rapid social change we are witnessing in Greece today make it unlikely that the modest expectations Athenian mothers nurture will find full satisfaction. Speaking from personal and professional experience, I would say that during late adolescence and early adulthood every painful step a young person takes in the direction of discovering the set of values and life style that suit him and his time best is a step away from his parents. It is very difficult indeed for a young person to question the parental values and way of life without negating, even temporarily, the parents themselves. It is equally difficult for parents to accept the adjustments their children make to new mores and customs without feeling threatened or even rejected. Yet it appears to be an almost inevitable part of modern day living for young persons—the most lively, creative and inquisitive of them at least—to be seeking new solutions to human problems.

This is both because new economic, social and political developments have rendered the traditional well tested models obsolete and also because the newer versions we, the first one or two generations of modern Athenians, have to offer are not very tempting to emulate. Even the mother–child relationship, the most solid of human bonds, has in the last couple of years suffered many debilitating blows that have changed it considerably; to the point where young girls today (at least most of the ones I have taught, counselled or befriended) are embarking upon the adventure of motherhood with the firm intention of adopting an approach different to that of their mothers'. In practice, however, they may soon find themselves replicating many of the maternal patterns, for they are starting off with the bitter–sweet taste of a tormented relationship they wish to avoid duplicating, but no knowledge of the conditions that brought it about. They hope to arrive at a formula, with more of this and less of the other, that will be better suited to the needs of modern people than the formula they were brought up with. Yet they appear to be overlooking the simple fact that any formula which is to be consumed in large doses must above all be palatable. For the formula of child-rearing to be judged as palatable it must consist of a pattern of daily interaction that is smooth and agreeable to both parties involved. A simple 'natural' pattern is required that is hard to attain in our denaturalized society.

When we speak of fragmentation and alienation and the many social evils of the modern way of life, I do not think we are aware exactly how limiting our mode of social organization is on each and every one of our human relations. At least I was not when I first embarked upon my career as a mother. Deprived as we are of experiences of communal living, we cannot see our individual case history as part of a larger whole nor can we compare our own behaviour to a group of other people like us. We have therefore no objective yardstick by which to assess our specific reality. Living in a near vacuum socially, we can be easily misled into nurturing over optimistic expectations about the future of our relations, passing extremely harsh judgement on ourselves and others when our expectations fail to be met. We pay lip service to the concept of alienation, but having mostly ourselves and our family to judge from we cannot very easily ascribe an objective meaning to the word. I had to see many urban mothers in their daily toil just to begin to understand that there are socially determined limits to the amount of satisfaction an urban woman can derive from her maternal role; and that these limits, restricted as they are, can only be reached with much continuous effort.

10 Epilogue

Having arrived at the end of my comparison between the traditional and the modern patterns of mother–child interaction, the obvious question to ask is what is in it for us today, just another pessimistic message that the quality of human exchange that once was is no longer attainable?

My aim from the start was to make a realistic assessment of the present situation and, if the comparison with the past does, in this domain, come out unfavourably on our side, we only have to take a longer view of history to see that our fate is not the hardest that ever was. It may be that the reason social critics tend to sound like doomsayers is because our generation was particularly ill-prepared to accept the kind of difficulties we are now facing. The political ideologies of the beginning of the century coupled with the technological explosion led us to believe that the best of two worlds was in store for us. We anticipated, and quite realistically so, that technological progress would pull us out of the state of material want in which our ancestors had lived for some millenia. We prepared ourselves for the political change that would put into practice the principles of democracy and socialism, contributing to a more egalitarian distribution of the newly acquired goods. But we assumed, unrealistically, that the enormous changes which these new developments entailed would take place without disturbing the quality of life we were enjoying until then and of which we were neither much aware nor very appreciative.

Not only in Greece but on the international scene as well the twentieth century was the century of great expectations. From politicians to artists and architects (as Huxtable, 1981, eloquently points out), we all believed we were entering a new era where material sufficiency would open the door to freedom, beauty and harmony. 'We believed', says Huxtable, 'that the world could be housed and fed; that we could bring order to our cities, . . . that the better life and the better world were finally within our grasp. We joined hands and sang, "We shall overcome"'. Now we have reached the point of almost total disillusionment, after having become painfully aware that the price of affluence is dear indeed. This price is to be paid both by those nations who are well out of need and want and by those (like us in Greece) who are barely emerging. The novel socio-economic structures which technological progress entails leave little room for beauty or harmony; either at the environmental level or at the level of human relations.

No matter how hard architects and planners try, our cities are becoming unfriendly, disorganized and most unattractive. No matter how much effort we invest in the conservation of the family institution, family bonds are weakening beyond control. Child rearing, as I believe I have illustrated in this book, is becoming an ungracious task; difficult to carry through from day to day and impossible to coat with long term expectations when existential continuity is threatened with disruption. Great as the maternal investment may be the spectre of loneliness is ever present, threatening each and every day the morrow and the distant future; just as the spectre of starvation had been threatening our ancestors for generations.

If the comparison of the rural and urban way of life that was undertaken in this book gave the impression that our ancestors led a better life than we do, this is due to the fact that the comparison focused exclusively on the realm of human relations; a domain that is commonly accepted as one of the weak points of our civilization. Surely, if the focus of the book was on hygiene or nutrition, material comfort, freedom of choice, leisure or political freedom, instead of mother–child interaction, the balance would have tilted in our direction.

The most important lesson I learned from my acquaintance with the traditional mode of life is how valuable a guide thorough knowledge of existing possibilities and limitations within a given culture really is. Unlike traditional communities, where long past experience offered the guidelines for each of life's occasions, our modern society finds itself deprived of the knowledge from the past that would make our complex world more predictable. The world we live in is not only infinitely more complex than the traditional one, but it is also quite unknown to us, for we only have a few years of comparable experience to rely back upon as opposed to the millenia that built traditional knowledge. Thanks to this clear knowledge of reality our rural ancestors succeeded in structuring a mode of life that did offer quite a few satisfactions within a minimum of resources available. People's expectations, goals and aspirations were shaped by the realistic assessment of existing possibilities; an assessment that was not based upon personal estimates, but on public opinion and tested common knowledge.

Today the aspirations each one of us nurtures are based on our personal estimates about the rewards available in a world one knows little about; the half truths, myths and generalities and the disjointed information presented to us through the mass media being the guidelines for our life's decisions, from the way we allot our efforts to the rewards we anticipate. To many of us daily life would have been a lot more acceptable if it were not for the distance separating it from some unrealistic vision we were led to nurture.

If our peasant or shepherd ancestor could be proud and contented in the material deprivation he lived in, this could well be due to the fact that he never hoped for more; for he knew all too well that within the boundaries of his homeland the only realistic aspiration was to stay beyond the threshold of starvation. There was no self-blame, guilt or feelings of inadequacy for a state of poverty which was known to be unavoidable. Instead of leading to fatalism, the realistic knowledge of the limited resources available galvanized a fighting spirit, self-esteem and co-operation. Our rural ancestors did try continuously and to the best of their ability, but without anger, without guilt and without illusions. Women did not blame their husbands, men did not accuse women, nor children their parents, for the poverty they all had to put up with. They accepted it knowingly as an inevitable part of life.

If only we knew the limitations which our culture imposes on us at the social-interpersonal level as clearly as the traditional people knew the economic constraints of their own culture, we would be in a better position than we are at present. Not that knowledge alone could much improve the mother–child or husband–wife relations, but much of the anger and guilt involved might give way to self-contentment and other-appreciation if the external adversity was realistically appraised. Unrealistic expectations are bound to leave us with a sense of failure, which we either bear alone corroding our self-esteem or we try to pass on to others (husband and offspring) turning the household into a battlefield, with mutual accusations as ammunition.

In this book I have tried to delineate some of the difficulties in parent–child relations I consider inherent to our way of life, in the belief that if we see them as such we shall lower our expectations and raise our sense of achievement proportionately.

If we accept the hard truth that our life is to be lived at the threshold of loneliness, just as those before us spent theirs at the threshold of hunger, then the fear of passing through this threshold might mobilize us to examine the whole structure of human relations more carefully. Where the limits are narrow the consequence of ignorance can be far reaching. There is no room for unbridled optimism in our age as far as human relations are concerned, but nor can we afford fatalistic pessimism. Under the present circumstances, the best we can aspire to is keeping above threshold level, and for this continuous effort is needed. It may be that if we dare face reality for what it is parents will also dare admit to themselves and to their children that, despite their efforts, what they have created as a family is not really much; it is only better than loneliness and this not as an admission of failure, but as a plain reality assessment. Instead of stubbornly trying to label as intimacy the often antagonistic forces that emerge within the modern family, passing the blame around from the one to the other, from mother to father and from parent to children and back again, we might just as well accept that in the social and interpersonal domain we are far behind our needs and longings.

Traditional rural people never thought of denying or hiding from their children the material deprivation they suffered. In fact they talked about it quite a lot, priding themselves that despite the depriving conditions they managed to secure the bare minimum. I wonder why we in contrast are so reluctant to admit how meagre the returns are in the social interpersonal domain despite our efforts.

Furthermore, if mothers really knew beforehand how few the possible rewards are in this role maybe they would weigh more carefully the other options open to them. Those who would decide for it would at this point have no reason to feel trapped in their role, as is often the case nowadays. It is quite surprising how, at a time when all issues are being discussed so openly, on motherhood there appears to be, in Greece that is, a conspiracy of silence. Although much has been said and written about partial problems, we appear to be evading the fundamental issue through fear of having to question some basic and long cherished assumptions. From the moment I began writing this book the same question kept repeating itself in my mind; a question I knew I could not avoid facing, but for which I had no answer either: given all the possibilities open to women today, is mothering a role that enriches or restricts a woman's life? And at what cost?

Most young women embark upon the adventure of motherhood with little foresight of the difficulties and impasses awaiting them; with no awareness of the absurdity involved in the efforts of a lone struggler trying to become an agent of socialization. With my present knowledge, having seen, experienced and understood the pains and disillusionments involved, would I be willing to become a mother if I were to start my life again? The only way I can answer this question is by quoting the French pilot who in January 1982 crossed the Atlantic on a surfing board: 'I am ever so glad and proud I did it, but I wouldn't do it again', not single-handedly that is. Certainly, of all the battles I have fought in my life that of rearing my two children had the most profound influence on my personality, and for this reason it is impossible for me to answer the question of mothering in the negative.

We are in an age when we are continuously led to think and act in terms of only our personal interests, where compulsive preoccupation with self-improvement (dieting, exercising, beautification, education, etc.) is reaching endemic proportions. Parenting appears to be the single most important humanizing experience open to the average intelligent person who cannot go against the current and find a plausible cause larger than himself to devote his life to. The young child's helplessness, his total dependence on his parents and his tremendous ability to create a strong impact on his environment, whenever in need, work as a most effective lever (almost the only one left in our individualistic competitive society) capable of expanding the limits of our ego boundaries to include another human being into a state of indivisible 'we-ness'.

Willingly or unwillingly, consciously or intuitively, a mother comes to adopt her child's perception as part of her own, looking at the world through her own eyes and those of her child at the same time. The power children have to affect adults, to move, annoy, irritate or hurt them whenever they are dissatisfied, mobilizes mothers to seek ways to alleviate this dissatisfaction. Thus, while their children are young and under their protection, mothers look at the environment, social and natural, in terms of potential sources of pleasure for their child. They naturally gravitate towards friends with same age children, select places for their outings in terms of potential entertainment and safety for their children and prepare foods that are palatable to the young. When they address their two-year-olds they use sentences barely more complex than the ones children themselves use; when at the beach they look out for colourful pebbles and shells; on the street they tend to notice dogs and cats passing by, big lorries and colourful tractors, and so on. They alter in the process their own identity and create a kind of bonding that is irreversible. This child orientation may vary in degree from one mother to another, being accompanied by enjoyment, resentment, frustration and acceptance in varying doses from case to case. Yet, whoever has experienced this total identification with another human being, no matter how much effort it entailed, has also experienced a fundamental change of personality on the social–emotional level, to the point where one can no longer perceive of oneself as independent of this experience. This might be one of the reasons for the mother to child bonding being so strong and long lasting.

Unfortunately, however, the social structure of our modern world appears to run counter to the fulfilment of the most basic of social human needs, like mothering, for example. This experience can only be gained through hard and ungracious effort and more often than not at the expense of the satisfaction of other important needs like self-ascertainment, social recognition and companionship. Furthermore, the rules of the social and economic game as played from school to corporation contribute to the development of strong boundaries around the individual that will protect him from his competitors, shield his own weaknesses and eventually isolate him from his fellow men. Thus, not only conflicting social roles, but to a certain extent the individual's own nature as well, as moulded by modern society, antagonize the human needs for parenthood and intimacy. When a woman enters motherhood while she is still young and malleable and has not yet developed strong and rigid ego boundaries she runs into one set of problems, when motherhood comes after the development of personal and professional identity she has a different set of problems to cope with. Either way, motherhood seldom if ever appears to be a smooth continuation of the life a woman had led previously.

To a young girl in her early twenties motherhood often means a break from real life before she has had a chance to savour it, before she is in a position to differentiate facts from fiction and come to grips with the negative side of freedom and independence. Before she discovers her own strengths and weaknesses, her likes and dislikes, before she has a chance to develop her personal criteria of what makes her feel good or bad, she is called to put aside all self-preoccupation to assume the role of the responsive caregiver. It is my impression that this early divergence from the road to self-discovery and differentiation often gives young women a sense of diminishment, particularly when they find little recognition for their child rearing task from their husband and relatives, in which case their sense of identity appears to suffer considerably. Furthermore, young mothers can, out of inexperience, easily fall into the trap of over-idealizing the lives of career women. They may compare their home bound existence, of which they have personal knowledge, with the fictitious notions they have formed, from piecing together the public images of successful professionals; images based on the half truths with which the mass media usually feed us in abundance.

On the other hand, the reality of a woman who becomes a mother after she has advanced somewhat in her career is not free of difficulties either. The shift of orientation required of her, in order to adjust to the demands of the new role, are likely to place a great strain on her. After several adult years spent as an independent agent, a thinker and doer in a competitive environ-ment, shifting to the role of the attentive listener constantly available to respond instead of initiating action must be hard indeed. What I am afraid of is that the continuous effort needed for this change of orientation takes a lot of the pleasure out of the daily routine of child care, especially during the early years. The later children arrive in a modern woman's life the harder her adjustment becomes, given the fact that modern life offers almost no opportunities for other-directed activity. Furthermore, the practical prob-lems of combining work and child care often render the difficulties inherent in this task almost insurmountable.

In both cases the struggle is difficult and the pleasures modest, with the end of the road—when the children come of age—leading to an almost inevitable and painful separation. This separation can hardly be faced realistically when parents, and mothers in particular, have invested so much in the relationship. It is very hard indeed for mothers in Athens today to accept that mothering is a role of limited duration, an occupation from which they will be called to retire possibly as early as the age of forty five; for when their children reach the age of twenty or twenty-two not only will their services be no longer needed, but not even their advice and direction. This unwillingness on the part of the young today to turn to their parents for guidance, which pains the elders considerably, often serves a good purpose. I tend to believe that one of the few roads leading to satisfaction in life is the road one chooses alone. The life our children are going to lead is going to be depriving in many ways, just as ours is. In our age of myths and ephemeral idols, no matter what life-model young people adopt it is bound to compare unfavourably with other models viewed from a distance under the lights of publicity. The best motivation for young people to fight effectively and with conviction is the knowledge that they are fighting their own battle; for those who are clearheaded and able enough to delineate their own course of action that is.

This close up view of mothering in our time—the practical difficulties of a lone performance, the short duration of the role, the price that must be paid in seclusion and the limited satisfaction that this role entails—offers to me at least ample evidence that child rearing can no longer constitute a woman's only goal in life. The fragmentation of functions, typical of our era, has restricted the breadth of most of life's expressions to such a degree that if people are to satisfy their varied needs for social recognition, intimacy, productivity and parenting they need to make considerable investment in more than one domain. The division of labour—men at work, women at home—is too restricting a specialization for all concerned, leaving important aspects of the human psyche unattended in both sexes. Most people, men and women alike, need a place in the labour force in order to assert their identity among peers and to feel a part of the social system. They also need an intimate and supportive relationship that will help them counterbalance the alienating competitive influences of the work situation and will satisfy their social and emotional needs.

These needs, which cannot be lightly ignored, cannot be satisfied in a home bound existence as was the case in the traditional rural villages. Today only professional activity and an intimate relation, a husband–wife relation for most people, can satisfy those needs. Under the present circumstances child rearing cannot become an end in itself, nor can it constitute a woman's exclusive life goal. The need for parenting must by necessity be realistically subordinated to the need for identity and social intimacy. Only as part and an outgrowth of a meaningful professional and marital experience can I see child rearing becoming an enriching experience. Just as for destitute people child bearing was a means of perpetuating the poverty cycle, similarly for lonesome people it is a means of perpetuating alienation.

If children, instead of being a woman's exclusive domain, separating and differentiating her activities from those of her husband's, became the couple's common task, child rearing might find again some of its lost meaning and pleasure. Co-operative parenting is for a woman probably the best way out of the ungracious role of solitary child-rearing and her seclusion from socio-economic life. For children also, now that collective effort is unattainable, this may be the only way for them to become socialized, by a co-operative effort that will provide them with a model, minimal as it may be, of human co-operation. For men as well this may be the best way to counteract the emotional deprivation to which their career orientation has condemned them. Maybe because as a child I had the opportunity to live close to a man who was the typical model of the successful male achiever, I am convinced that the man who in our age invests all his efforts in one domain—the advancement of his career—ends up, no matter how successful he may be, with a longing for human contact and intimacy. This longing, that only a child's intuition can discern behind the bravado and the exhilaration of fame and achievement, is a profound unsatisfied need for the kind of human relations which can only be achieved through mutual effort and the pursuit of a common task. They never come as a bonus to professional success as many achievers would have liked to believe.

Both men and women need the close collaboration. It is as much of a fallacy for a man to believe that he can channel all his energy into his work as it is for a woman to believe she can rear her children single-handedly. In the end they will probably both find themselves equally empty-handed.

Recently in the United States there have been several attempts at co-operative child-rearing by father and mother, on the basis of equal responsibility, with both parents reorganizing their professional commitments to fit in with child-rearing demands. I can see many advantages to this solution, both as a way of strengthening the husband-wife relationship and as a means of easing the task of child-rearing. I can also see the innumerable difficulties that such a collaborative approach would entail, not only in Greece, where cultural obstacles would make it almost impossible to carry through, but in the more developed countries as well where it is beginning to gain ground.

It is not my intention to present co-operative child-rearing as *the* answer to the problem of mothering. For one thing I have no knowledge of the ongoing pioneer efforts and for another I do not believe that there can be any easy or permanent solution to problems of human relations in our time; solutions which can help us leave the spectre of solitude securely behind us, enriching our human relations with the strength and depth of old. Only as a potential option of action do I suggest collaborative parenting as a way out of the impasse of mothering as a solitary endeavour. It is an illustration of the only type of approach I consider promising: an approach that acknowledges that the difficulties of child-rearing in our time are greater than a lone person can handle, while at the same time clearly drawing from modern reality in a quest for modern patterns of interaction, instead of merely replicating models that resemble the traditional ones in form while being mere parodies in essence.

My basic belief, which I have tried to present throughout this book, is that as long as our mode of production remains individualistic no stable social groupings can exist. Without a stable social frame interpersonal relations will be brittle and precarious. Under the existing circumstances we can only speak of techniques designed to facilitate and sustain parent–child and husband–wife relations, some possibly more successfully than others, but not of a remedy that will cure the alienation typical of our era.

Human relations today cannot offer all they used to and mothering can no longer be what is was. Without self-deceit or guilt let us allow ourselves to face this reality, to experience fully the loss, the disillusionment, the emptiness. Let us mourn the death of interdependence, cohesiveness, stability and continuity in human relations and after we have buried our dead let us turn to our modern world and look at the alternative ways that are open to us for gaining interpersonal satisfaction. Our heritage compels us to hold on to human relations as an essential part of life, but only in the present can we find the viable patterns that will sustain these relations. If we accept that the ready-made models and opportunities modern life offers for intimacy and meaningful human exchange amount to almost zero then we shall by necessity look for new interpersonal schemata new techniques of communication and eventually a new life model.

Friendships, love affairs, books, teachings, counsellings, doubts, trials and errors, let us be open and experience them all searchingly and questioningly for as long as youth gives us the stamina we need to bear the insecurity of search. Only thus can we lay our hands on some of the few 'nutrients' available in our socially depriving world with which to put together, step by step, a modern yet substantial life model. Small as these steps may be, as long as they are real and need no myths to sustain them they will offer the little daily interpersonal pleasures that, to us Greeks, make even the most modest of lives worth living.

Appendix I: Historical Survey of the Rural Greek Milieu

The intention behind the brief historical survey attempted here is not to provide a condensed history of the Greek rural people. The aim instead is briefly to sketch the historical framework against which a particular form of socio-economic organization gradually evolved. In other words, it is an attempt to clarify what historical necessity originally gave rise to the specific cultural patterns observed in this milieu today, what needs these patterns were originally designed to meet and to what extent these needs still exist today.

The history of modern Greece is typical of the fate of small nations evolving in the periphery of the modern world; the country's rise of national consciousness, its claims for political independence, economic and social autonomy, being intertwined with the interests the superpowers had vested in the area.

The geographical area now called modern Greece constituted for nearly two millenia an agglomerate of semi-independent, mostly agrarian settlements, greatly influenced in their development by the rise and decline of multinational empires of which they were a part. Part of the Byzantine empire for about 1000 years, they were annexed to the Ottoman empire in 1453. Until 1821, when the struggle for independence resulted in the formation of the modern Greek state, the villages and small towns spread across the Hellenic land did not form a nation in the modern sense. The limited interconnection between the villages, coupled with the direct links many of the settlements developed with one or more of the empire's large urban centres, led to the development of distinct localities and strong local consciousness. The analysis of any aspect of Greek social reality should be coupled with the understanding that Greek settlements have been for several centuries ecosystems with open boundaries, that is open to the oppression and opportunities afforded by their interrelation with multinational socio-political and economic forces.

A. The Byzantine and Ottoman heritage

An endless conflict between the emperor's central government and the local landlords marks the entire Byzantine era; a conflict which was never resolved in favour of the lords as in Western Europe. Byzantium, like most Eastern empires, was organized on the basis of a dual social structure: (a) the small farmers organized in a family and community system in the countryside; (b) the centralized administration in the cities, with taxation as the link connecting these two separate worlds. The absence of any rigid system of social stratification gave the Byzantine administration a worldly-popular character that clearly differentiated it from Western societies (Runciman, 1952; Vergopoulos, 1975). The cornerstone of the Byzantine state was the freedom and autonomy of the small-scale agricultural producers. The main source of income and the largest part of the imperial army were provided by the peasantry. It was, therefore, quite natural that the emperor should steadily support his peasants from the arbitrariness of the powerful local lords (Vergopoulos, 1975) from expropriations and debts. The strengthening of the feudal lords beyond the emperor's control marks the beginning of the decline of the Byzantine empire (Vergopoulos, 1975).

Several historians (Kordatos, 1964; Vakalopoulos, 1964; Vergopoulos, 1975) noted that, under the pressure of the local lords and the erratic policies of the central authorities, the Byzantine peasants tended to view the Ottoman conquerors as the liberators who would protect them from the tyranny of the local powers. 'The expansion of the Ottoman empire over the Byzantine world can be viewed as providing a finite and radical solution to the conflict between the wealthy landowners and the peasants, a conflict which for the last three centuries had led the Byzantine empire to an impasse' (Vergopoulos, 1975, p. 55). The Ottoman conquest took, in the beginning at least, the form of an agrarian reform that curtailed the power of all noblemen and improved considerably the lot of the peasants during the 15th and 16th centuries. In summarizing the agrarian production system under the Ottoman empire, three important features stand out: (1) the freedom allowed the peasants, (2) the family system of land cultivation and (3) the cohesiveness and autonomy of the rural communities. As a general rule the land belonged to the state; the peasants managed small family lots, given to them by the state, which would stay in the family from one generation to the next and could neither be appropriated by the state nor sold by the peasants.

Between the state and the peasants a class of civil servants (timariots) was interpolated, responsible for the collection of taxes and the recruitment of men for the army. The peasant although in form only a mere land tenant— since private ownership was unknown to the Ottomans—was *de facto* a landowner, since he payed no rent to the state or to any private individual. The state took over the agricultural surplus through taxation, but this impersonal state of affairs would allow the peasant total freedom of action. *Vis-à-vis* the state, the community as a whole was taxable and not the individuals. The eventual failure of one member to pay his share had to be met by the other community members (Vergopoulos, 1975, p. 61). As a result a communal solidarity developed in the countryside, which was directly related to the development of a centralized government in the cities (Pantazopoulos, 1967). As long as the community paid its taxes to the state it had few other obligations towards the central government and was allowed complete judicial, religious, economic and political power over its own members (Vergopoulos, 1975; Fotiadis, 1958). Some communities in forested areas had to keep local guards and the island and litoral populations had to give the Turkish fleet a certain number of sailors. The most adverse imposition on the Christian population, however, was the recruitment of children from the ages of six to fifteen to be trained for the Turkish army.

In the course of the 17th and 18th centuries, the halting of the Empire's westward expansion into Europe, and indeed the beginning of the slow but steady retreat of the Empire from Europe, cut at the very roots of an imperial system based on military expansion and colonization. The loss of territory in Europe resulted in a serious loss of manpower and tax revenues, which aggravated the already serious economic problems facing the Empire. 'It was the Porte's (State Government) chronic shortage of money that contributed to the institutionalization of extortion and rapacity at all levels of society' (Clogg, 1973, p. 4). One consequence of this development was the collapse of the Ottoman Empire as a unitary state and the growth of provincial autonomies in many regions of the Empire characterized by the emergence of a new provincial and often ruthless elite.

During this period, dramatic tax increases, manslaughter, warfare and looting of the Christian communities led the majority of Greek peasants to abandon the plains and to withdraw to the mountainous regions or to migrate west (Svoronos, 1976; Moskof, 1974). It is during this period that the institution of the ciftlik (extended land ownership) came into effect. 'The ciftlik marks the transition from a social and economic structure founded upon a system of moderate land rent and few labour services to one of excessive land rent and exaggerated service' (Clogg, 1973, p. 4). One consequence of this development was that the proprietor of a ciftlik village often received from his peasants as much as one half of the produce after they had paid the land tax to the state (Stoianovich, 1953). The ciftliks emerged primarily in the fertile plains of Thessaly, in Euboia, in a small part of Epirus and in Attica, that is primarily in the regions which had been abandoned by the persecuted peasants who took to the mountains (Vergo-poulos, 1975). Yet according to Tsoukalas (1977), at no point during the Ottoman Empire did the ciftliks expand to occupy more than a fifteenth to a twentieth of the agrarian population.

Even within the context of the 'feudal' system of rural production, however, land cultivation remained a purely family enterprise. The farmer was not a hired hand; he cultivated together with his family the same piece of land from year to year and from generation to generation, giving the landowner up to 50% of the products in return for the land use. The landowner had no right to expel the farmers from the land, nor could he monopolize the returns from an increase in the land production (Vergo-poulos, 1975). Up until 1889 the regulation manuals dictating the mutual rights and obligations of the farmers *vis-à-vis* the landowner were not drafted on an individual basis; the entire village community constituted the one party and the landowner the other. The landowners, like the Porte had done before them, collected their revenues from each village in toto and not from individual farmers.

As a general conclusion, it can be stated that the Greek peasant from the time of the Byzantine Empire to the beginning of the modern Greek state in 1830 had lived and worked under conditions of relative freedom and independence in a family-oriented economy, under the control and protection of a tightly knit village community, where the Church played an all-important role.

B. The years 1830–1920

In the course of the 150 years that elapsed from the foundation of the modern Greek state to the present day, Greece as a whole, and the rural milieu in particular, has been through several major crises—wars, internal strifes, dictatorships, the rise and fall of the monarchy, earthquakes, etc. Yet, despite the dramatic changes brought about during this period, the development of modern cities, the progressive industrialization of the country and the massive invasion of western values, the traditional form of rural production and consequently the basic structure of the rural Greek milieu, have retained a surprising degree of stability. The small rural family enterprise has not only survived, but has prevailed as the economically viable form of agricultural enterprise par excellence, and the village community, although stripped of much of its legal and administrative authority, remained all-important in regulating the normative behaviour of its members until quite recently.

In the first 90-year-period (1830–1920), four major developments can be said to have influenced directly the Greek rural milieu: (1) the national lands distribution, (2) the agrarian reform, (3) the great exodus (urbanization and immigration) and (4) the mercantilist shift of agricultural production.

(a) The national lands distribution and the rural reform

During the Turkish occupation the largest proportion of Greek arable land belonged to the Turkish government—a certain part had been distributed to the Church, the monasteries, Turkish officials and Greek men of wealth. According to Tsoukalas (1977), at the time of Greek independence in 1830 about 30–40% of Greek land was privately owned, while the remaining 60–70%, which belonged to the Turkish state, was—according to the international treaty that recognized the independence of the Greek state—proclaimed 'national property'. The farming and exploitation of the national lands, which represented over 50% * of the arable land and which naturally included the most fertile areas of the country, became one of the country's hottest political issues for nearly a century.

Despite the serious pressure exerted by the wealthy landowners on the state authorities to sell the national lands, the Greek state chose to nationalize the land and rent it on a permanent basis to the farmers who would cultivate it. In its final form, the land reform divided the national lands into small family properties which were distributed to the farmers. But the distribution of the national lands did not offer a satisfactory answer to the problems of the entire agrarian population, for during that period nearly 40% of the farmers were based in the privately owned ciftliks (Vergopoulos, 1975). The liberal stand of the Venizelos government, coupled with the strengthening of the middle classes, created the prerequisite for a land reform that would drastically curtail the privileges of the landowners in favour of the farmers. The Venizelos measures against the ciftlik lords were partly dictated by the government's policy to facilitate industrialization by diverting private investments from the land to industry. In 1917 the land reform was announced. It limited the size of the land that could be privately owned and distributed the surplus to the landless farmers. Undoubtedly, the one factor that precipitated the implementation of the land reform was the war in Asia Minor, with the resultant 1 200 000 refugees who flooded the Greek countryside in 1922.

In conclusion, it can be noted that, at the end of the first 100 years of the newly founded Greek state, the traditional family-owned agricultural enter-

---

* The figures are quite debatable, ranging from 50–35% (Vergopoulos, 1975, p. 109).

prise was an ingrained feature of the rural milieu, which it dominated. It was not evident as a relic of the past, but as the most suitable mode of rural production within the frame of rising urbanization and industrialization; it appeared to be a mode of production that would secure for the state maximal returns in terms of products (through hard human labour) with minimal capital investment.

(b) The great exodus

From the fall of the Byzantine empire to the present day, a large percentage of Greeks have lived outside the boundaries of Greece. They organized themselves into communities and exerted an important influence both on the host countries and on the mother land. During the whole of the 18th and 19th centuries, the steady flow of emigration from the rural villages towards the cities and abroad was one of the determining factors that helped shape the Greek milieu in general and the rural communities in particular. Yearly, large segments of the rural population left their homeland for the prosperous communities of Rumania, southern Russia, Asia Minor, Egypt and even central Africa, where their fellow countrymen prospered through commerce and trade. This continuous flow of emigration helped to expand the range of activity of these Greek communities and kept the strong ties between the emigrants and the homeland. The steady flow of income that was pouring into the rural communities, coupled with a relative decrease of the rural population, was one of the main factors perpetuating small farm ownership (Tsoukalas, 1977, p. 23). It is interesting to note that the majority of rural emigrants came from the areas where the small family enterprise prevailed (Tsoukalas, 1977).

Given the corporate nature of the rural family enterprise and the limited size of the arable land available, it becomes apparent that a population increase would result in a decrease of per capita income. Therefore, finding a means of controlling a population explosion was of tantamount importance. One way of controlling the number of farmers per family, while expanding and differentiating the range of bread-winning activities and thus increasing the family income, was through migration. For the Greek peasants, as opposed to most other immigrants from the Mediterranean basin, immigration whether abroad or to the cities did not mean abandonment of the family enterprise; on the contrary, it was an important means of strengthening it (Tsoukalas, 1977). The USA immigration statistics—which are one of the few reliable sources of information on the Greek immigrants— offer important information about the immigrants' homeward orientation as a Greek phenomenon. 'Between the years 1908–1930, 61% of the Greek immigrants returned to their homeland; an enormous percentage when compared to other ethnic groups, who appeared to break off completely with their native country once settled in the USA. The yearly remittances sent by Greeks back home amounted to $50 per person, as compared to $32 for the Italians, $28 for the English and Irish and $4.05 for the Germans' (Tsoukalas, 1977, pp. 152–53).

The development of a family network outside the confines of the family territory served a number of purposes directly related to the survival of the family group. Not only did it alleviate the pressures on the family enterprise, by limiting the number of people to be fed by the land revenues, but it increased the family income, mentioned above, by channelling some of its members into more profitable activities outside agriculture. It also secured access to new economic outlets for the entire family, should the need arise. The immigrants in any given milieu, whether in the Greek cities or abroad, served as a connecting link between the village and the more prosperous urban communities in Greece and abroad. The emigration of one family member abroad opened the road for other members of the family to move in the same direction (Tsoukalas, 1977). In fact the entire village community would profit from the established link, as well as the members of the family. As noted by Constantinidis (in Tsoukalas, 1977), wealthy Greek merchants abroad would play a paternal role towards all emigrants coming from their native village, finding employment for them either in their own business or guiding them to start their own small enterprises. Thus we find during the 18th and 19th centuries several Greek communities in Egypt, in Asia Minor, in Central Europe and in the USA, which are populated almost exclusively by the inhabitants of one island or one village (Moskof, 1974). If the relatives and compatriots back in the village gained in terms of material returns and security by having a member of their ingroup well settled abroad, the emigrants themselves must have benefited equally by the perpetuation of the links with their native land. Undoubtedly, it takes a well-balanced mutual interest to keep alive from generation to generation, for over a century, the bonds that linked a great number of Greek villages with specific Greek communities abroad. 'In communities with a high rate of emigration we find a surprising number of hospitals, old people's homes, welfare funds, schools, orphanages, scholarship funds, all coming from donations from successful emigrants' (Tsoukalas, 1977, p. 128).

(c) The mercantilist shift of agricultural production

At the time of the foundation of the modern Greek state, the agricultural production in the majority of villages had the character of a closed system of economy geared primarily to self-sufficiency. Goods were exchanged among the families in the community or among neighbouring villages. Sugar and coffee were about the only items purchased from the outside world, in exchange for a minimum of surplus products. The transition from this closed system of economy to trade-oriented agricultural production was brought about quite gradually. The main tactic used by the state in order to draw the agricultural surplus into the cities and additionally to force the farmers to increase their production—and therefore the marketable surplus—was through taxation (Vergopoulos, 1975; Tsoukalas, 1977). Around 1917, the farmers paid over 50% of the state taxes. The Ottoman tradition had accustomed the peasants to paying high rates of taxation and their reaction to the Greek state, when it followed the same practices, took on extreme forms only during the years of poor harvest.

Around 1880, agricultural products began to appear on the market on a large scale. The return of the farmers to the plains, after the national lands distribution, coincided with a broadening of the spectrum of agricultural production to including goods for export (Tsoukalas, 1977). In Greece, like in many developing countries, taxation was the most effective means of transforming agricultural production which was geared to self-consumption into commercially oriented production. Additionally, through the institution of agricultural loans, the state could indirectly exert considerable pressure on the farmers.

Despite this important change in agricultural production, the accelerated growth of the merchant class and the economic squeeze of the farmers, the structure of land ownership remained unchanged. 'The small family enterprise showed a remarkable degree of resistance to the debilitating influences of continuously increasing taxation, debts and exploitation from the city merchants' (Tsoukalas, 1977, p. 95). Only by referring to the particular socio-economic structure of the rural communities, the immigration policy resulting in demographic stability and the endless socio-psychological resources of the rural family, can we account for this unusual phenomenon of the stability of the small family enterprise in the midst of continuous adversity and change.

C. The period 1950–1970

It is well beyond the scope of this very brief survey to attempt to cover the period from 1940 to 1950, a period marked by a world war and a civil war. The fact that the class which won the civil war has ruled Greece up until the present day, imposing a heavy censorship on all historical accounts of this period—an attitude which only began to loosen up after 1974—makes an objective account of the period totally impossible without exhaustive research. Fully understanding the importance of this omission, the last part of the survey will only attempt a brief exposé of the socio-economic reality of the rural scene in our days.

Despite the massive exodus from the villages to the cities and the accelerated rate of emigration, affecting primarily the rural population, the number of agricultural enterprises between the years 1950–1971 remained stable (Vergopoulos, 1975). The overwhelming majority of enterprises are small and medium sized family enterprises. In 1971 independent family labour accounted for 92.55% of the active rural manpower (National Statistical Bulletin, 1972). While the number of family enterprises has remained stable the actual number of farmers has decreased (National Statistical Bulletin, 1972), a fact that indicates that the number of emigrants per family has increased.*

Between the years 1955–1971, over 1 500 000 farmers left the countryside; 60% of them, that is 900 000 people, took the road to Germany and other developed countries while the remaining 40%, i.e. 600 000 people, migrated to the cities in Greece. Taking into consideration the total rural population of Greece, it becomes apparent that in the years 1951–1970 Greek agriculture lost a third of its manpower (Vergopoulos, 1975). If the number of family enterprises remained stable despite this tremendous exodus, it is mainly because the migrating peasant very rarely sells his land; he rents it or gives it to a relative to cultivate for his own benefit. If a part of his immediate family remains in the village, he sends a large part of his wages to help them out (Peristiany, 1968; Vergopoulos, 1975).

During the early seventies the rural Greek family (owning some 3.42 hectares of land) appeared particularly well equipped with machinery and the mode of cultivation was intensive in most areas. As a result, the output of agricultural products increased by 50% between the years 1961 and 1970 (Avdelidis, 1974). From this, we may infer that the rural family enterprise continues to show a striking ability to adjust, adopting with the greatest ease all means of possible advancement, while retaining on the social level the traditional kinship structure. What appears to be almost unbelievable is the decrease in the prices of agricultural products during this twenty year period. At a period when the cost of living had gone up in most sectors of the economy, the yearly increase of revenues from agriculture was one quarter of the increase in volume; between the years 1961 and 1970, there was a 4.3% increase of volume of agricultural products and a 1.1% increase of revenue (Vergopoulos, 1975, p. 235). The state control of prices of agricultural products resulted in an increased pressure on the farmer to keep on producing more and more in order to meet the price increase in all the items he purchased, electricity, oil, machinery, clothing, etc. This pressure

---

* The birth rate during this period remained stable.

resulted in the bankruptcy of the farming enterprise as a profit-making endeavour, the immigration of most of the able members and the overwork of those who remained in the fields. The Greek farmer, while working much harder and much longer hours than most urban dwellers, was deep in debt and could just secure a low daily wage for all the working members of his family. It is no wonder that the number of large scale capitalist agricultural enterprises is minimal in Greece today, as no western type entrepreneur would choose to invest money in the agricultural production where the returns are minimal and profit non-existent.

During the late seventies, with the prospect of the country joining the European Common Market, a marked improvement in government policy towards farmers and their products was noted. It is doubtful, however, whether any government policy implemented at this stage could alter the course of events, and halt the massive exodus to the cities. On the one hand, the materialist values of a consumer society are now permeating every village community, through the mass media and increased mobility. In comparison to the opulent (as it appears from afar) city life, the hard work and asceticism demanded of village dwellers becomes questionable. On the other hand, the flexibility and readiness of the rural Greek people to explore new outlets for financial improvement outside the village confines, which operated for centuries as a safety valve for the survival of the villages, is now having the opposite effect (the opportunities having multiplied), leading to the gradual death of many villages, through desertion and marasmus. We are probably witnessing the end of the rural family enterprise, a system of production which has survived for over one thousand years and has safeguarded the continuity and identity of the whole nation.

Viewed in retrospect, the history of the Greek people is the history of a poor and oppressed but not dejected or fatalistic people. The richness, variety and quality of folk art present in almost every region of Greece, encompassing all forms of human activity (architecture, metal work, wood carving, pottery embroidery, weaving, dance, music, myths and legends), testifies to the vitality of the people and their institutions. Undoubtedly, the particular historical conditions operating in the Greek milieu for most of its history resulted in continuous adversity, which was, however, within tolerable limits often operating as a challenge for the people rather than a calamity. This mobilized people to use all their individual and collective resources in a continuous effort not only to cope with, but even to surmount poverty and adversity. The major factors contributing to the vigour of the rural communities are, I believe, first and foremost the amount of social and economic autonomy they enjoyed throughout the centuries. The fact that economic oppression took the form of taxation drawn on a moderate percentage basis of the total land products and exported handicrafts allowed the peasants an incentive for improving production. The central government's minimal interference with local affairs left with the people the ultimate responsibility for their progress and development. Secondly, the collective way of dealing with authority strengthened group cohesiveness, making the village community a kind of buffer between the family and external adversity, be it political and economic oppression or natural catastrophes. Thirdly, the opportunities for development afforded to the fittest through migration operated as a stabilizing force, revitalizing at the same time the rural communities. Undoubtedly, the structure of the Ottoman empire, loose as it was, facilitated to some extent the flow of internal migration. Along with economic sanctions, Ottoman rule brought to the Greek people added possibilities for development.

Neither history nor nature have been generous to the people of Greece, but they have not been unbearably harsh either. Great calamities (wars, looting, earthquakes, snowstorms, etc.) have been frequent, but of short duration, allowing people time to recuperate in-between. The equilibrium between the oppressing and galvanizing influence exerted by exernal political and economic forces appears to have remained stable throughout history in the Greek milieu overall. Individual communities have gone through phases of bloom and marasmus due to especially favourable or extenuating circumstances, but viewed as a whole Greek rural communities have for several centuries stood strong against adversity. This has produced in the process a mature culture perpetuated through stable institutions and reflected in the austere beauty of the man-made environment. Now, for the first time in two millenia of history, the advent of technological progress appears to mark a point of no return for the Greek villages. External social and economic forces are radically transforming the people and their communities, rather than being gradually assimilated by them and used to their advantage.

Appendix II: Historical Survey of the Development of the Modern Greek Metropolis

A. The structure of the newly-founded modern Greek state

It is almost tragic to note that the very same forces that secured the survival of the Greek peasantry for over a millenium, safeguarding its autonomy and its sense of nationality, hindered the development of an autonomous Greek state, from the beginning of its foundation to the present day.

The generous amount of freedom enjoyed by the Greeks during the 400 years of the Ottoman rule allowed the formation of 'miniature republics', as Dakin (1973) calls them, throughout the provincial scene. 'It was there that the lawless men of Greece, who among themselves observed strict codes of honour and duty, learned their patriotism—their loyalty to their locality (patrida), faith, families and patrons.' It was this patriotism and loyalty to their patrons which operated as a vital factor in bringing about the War of Independence and at the same time hindered the development of the Greek nation state. Militarily, the war was fought largely in terms of local self-government and on local funds (Dakin, 1973). But when the local leaders of the major regions of Greece—the Peloponnese, Western Greece, Eastern Greece and the Islands—were to agree among themselves on the general strategy of the war or later on the form of central government, any attempt at collaboration took the form of a power struggle.

The agrarian nature of the Greek economy and the complete absence of a Western type middle class of urban industrial producers did not necessitate the existence of a nation as a central coordinator of economic activity (Filias, 1974). The Greek state did not emerge gradually in response to specific local needs; it was not created *for* certain reasons, but primarily *against* a common enemy. The people revolted against oppression and exploitation, per-sonified primarily by the Turks, but also against the Greek primates. They wanted less taxation and less exploitation but they did not basically need a powerful central state; their local agricultural communities were autonomous enough both socially and economically not to warrant central control, at least at that stage of their development. The merchants-primates, to the extent they were interested, which was only marginally, 'were moved to throw their weight behind the struggle for independence by their increasing impatience with the arbitrariness and uncertainty that characterized Ottoman rule and which obviously stood in the way of the maximization of profits' (Clogg, 1973, p. 15). Foreign powers (France, England and Russia) saw in the Greek struggle for independence an opportunity to curtail the Ottoman influence. The intelligentsia, finally, seemed to be moved by an idealistic and nostalgic wish to bring back Greece's past glories (Clogg, 1973), totally unfounded in the local reality.

About three years after the outbreak of the revolution, it had become quite clear to all parties involved that the various sectors of society each pushed for independence with different aims and intentions; and the newly-founded government became an arena for local and class struggles where each group was after maximal gains. Eventually the old wealthy landowners and the rich Greeks 'of diaspora' (living abroad) became the absolute rulers of the local and national political scene and their people staffed the state machinery. The centralized government, which was formed under the Bavarians, contributed to the total extinction of any form of local political, administrative and economic autonomy (Filias, 1974). As a result, all problems without any exception, from minor to major, could only be met at the centre, that is, in Athens. Even before the final outcome of the revolution, the peasants who had contributed the most came to realize that not much would change regardless of the outcome. Heavy taxation, oppression, arbitrariness of decision, the oriental opulence of the wealthy few, the waste of foreign loans and the swiftness of the landlords in grabbing the Turkish estates had thoroughly demoralized the masses.

The social dynamics of the newly-founded state may be summarized as follows: the overall population, comprising primarily peasants with strong regional attachments, both social and economic, had no national consciousness other than a vague concept of Greekness as a religious and anti-Turkish sentiment. To this class the central government represented an alien body— since it was in the hands of the wealthy oligarchy—that had offered them nothing and had stripped them of much of the local autonomy they had enjoyed in the past. The only way for the peasants to gain access to the all-important central authority was indirectly through the network of personal contacts and ingroup affiliations, which had traditionally proven so effective. The link could be established either through the local patrons who were in the government or by sending members of the family in the capital to work for the great employer, the government (Tsoukalas, 1977). To the wealthy merchants and landowners state politics represented the means for the advancement of their family interests and a way of strengthening their local influence.

Within the first few years after the end of the revolution, the ruling class of wealthy merchants and landowners left their locality and moved into Athens, leaving behind a relative or representative to cultivate their interests and influence in their native district. In this way a system of political influences was created, called the system of political clientele. Country people—and later on city people as well—would give their vote in return for acquired or promised benefits and not for any ideological or party loyalty. With the vote being about the only 'privilege' accorded to the people by the state, it is only natural that Greeks would try and get the most out of it in terms of material benefits (Meynaud, 1965). Since the most valued 'favour' for a Greek peasant family was a job opportunity for one of its members, the class of the primates who in the past offered the opportunities for migration, with their rise to power in state politics, shifted to securing for their fellow countrymen positions in the civil service. By the end of the 19th century, Greece appears to have had the highest percentage of civil servants in the world.

The internal wave of migration was primarily directed to the capital, which grew disproportionately larger than any other Greek city. At the end of the 19th century, Athens was the largest city in the Balkans despite the fact that the population of Yugoslavia was double and that of Rumania three times larger than that of Greece. In the years 1800–1920, the Athenian population was multiplied 45 times, that of Bucharest 9 times, of Belgrade 4 times and Sofia 3 times (Weber, 1968). Thus it can be safely concluded that in Greece the percentage of urbanization in the capital was greater than in any other Balkan state.

The two main characteristics of the urbanization process in Greece up until 1920 were: (a) the growth of the capital, paralleled with the stagnation of other cities, and (b) the non-productive nature of the economy in the capital. The cumulative population increase of 15 Greek towns, between the years 1889–1907, was 7000 inhabitants, and for Athens alone 102 000 (Tsoukalas, 1977, p. 179). The civil services and the state functions being the main target of the urban immigrants, Athens soon became a most unusual city where state functions appeared to be the only 'raison d'être' of a population of 20 000 people.

The personalized character of Greek leadership resulted in a steadily ineffective governmental policy, characterized by a total absence of any long-term planning, a constant turnover of persons and interests and a mercantile profiteering plutocratic economy (Filias, 1974; Tsoukalas, 1977;

Moskof, 1974; Rodakis, 1975). The political game was played between the three powerful factions of the ruling class: the local merchants-landlords, the merchants 'of diaspora' and the throne, occasionally on a personal-family basis and occasionally on a class basis, but always by default of the people. A general state policy could be articulated and implemented only to the extent that it coincided with the interests of the three factions; when it conflicted with local or personal interests it was undermined. Similarly, the absence of almost any viable industry until about 1950 (Campbell and Sherrard, 1968), despite the considerable amount of capital imported into the country (Tsoukalas, 1977), the gradual marasmus of the countryside (Vergopoulos, 1974), the meagre investments allotted to the development of any infrastructure both technical (roads, transport, power plants, etc.) and social (education, medical care, etc.) (Rodakis, 1975), are but a few of the consequences and indications of the gross mismanagement of public affairs.

The Greeks 'of diaspora', who controlled in essence the country's social and economic life, set the tone and standards which were to prevail in the Greek socio-economic scene up to the present day. Mercenaries by tradition, alien to their home country, the Greeks 'of diaspora' saw their business enterprises as short-term profit-making endeavours based on the privileges obtained from the central government which they themselves controlled. The competition between the 'big families' for privileges and the changeable political scene, resulting in a rapid turnover of favourites, excluded any prospect of long-term investment policies, both at the level of individual enterprise and of state planning. If local ties led wealthy landlords to resist and undermine planning policies on a national level, the economic ties of the Greeks 'of diaspora' with the powers of the West prevented them from even conceptualizing a national policy independent—to the extent possible—of the interests of their host countries in the West. So deeply embedded was the notion of dependence in the ruling class consciousness that the only source of disagreement was in respect to the particular power which was to be the favoured one. The political parties that did emerge around 1830 differentiated their platforms on this issue and were actually named after their patrons, the English, the French and the Russian party. This lack of national consciousness on the part of the ruling class coupled with the non-existence of a middle class, as Filias (1974) noted, appears to have played a determining role in the socio-economic development of modern Greece. The unbridgeable gap (social, educational and economic) separating the privileged ruling class from the peasants (who up to 1922 constituted the overwhelming majority of the Greek population) gave the former complete freedom and unaccountability in the management of public affairs. The absence of a middle class left the Greeks 'of diaspora' unchallenged in the course of national development they set, motivated by their own economic interests.

Additionally, this cultural gap between the two sectors of Greek society can help explain the dissociation often noted between the Greek people and its rulers (Filias, 1974; Moskof 1974; Rodakis 1975). It can also explain the vigour with which the Utopian vision of Hellenism (the revival of the ancient Greek glory) was endorsed by the ruling class. This Utopian notion, which developed in the scholarly circles of the West, grew with great vigour when transplanted back to Greece (Campbell and Sherrard, 1968); firstly because it was an imported and therefore respectable 'product' and secondly because it allowed the Greeks 'of diaspora' to cherish a Greek ideal, while ignoring the reality of the Greek people, their needs and aspirations.

B. The growth of the Athenian working class 1830–1922

The first 90 year period after the foundation of the modern Greek state was marked by a significant economic growth, which did not correspond, however, to any considerable increase of the local production power. Although the gross national product increased three-fold between the years 1830 and 1920, most of the capital was imported and was consumed or absorbed by short-term profiteering, rather than being invested in productive enterprises. Foreign loans, immigrants' remittances and capital imported by the Greeks 'of diaspora' were the main sources of national income, supporting the ever-increasing number of unproductive urban dwellers (Tsoukalas, 1977).

Up to about 1870, the Greeks 'of diaspora' kept their business activities in the host countries, importing into Greece the surplus of their profits. This imported capital they partly spent in donations for public welfare and partly consumed in acquiring elegant mansions, importing luxury items and securing the services that would offer them a life cycle similar to the western European ruling class prototypes.

Up to this period Athens was so to speak a two class city, with elegant mansions housing the Greeks 'of diaspora' and the local landowners and comfortable if modest houses for the civil servants and their families. Neither slums nor barracks were anywhere to be seen (Tsoukalas, 1977). The largest fraction of the population represented the families of the place-holders and the place-hunters at humble levels in the government administration. There was also a growing class of shop-keepers and artisans serving this rather incongruous society (Campbell and Sherrard, 1968). After 1870, the growing international economic competition led the Greeks 'of diaspora' to transfer their business enterprises to their home country.

Native entrepreneurs and Greek merchants from abroad were now willing to invest capital in productive as well as commercial enterprises, greatly supported by a tailor-made policy of tariff protection (Tsoukalas, 1977). Despite serious financial and political risks, Greece experienced a considerable expansion of her economy during the last four decades of the nineteenth century, coupled by a considerable expansion of the world of professionals and salaried clerks working in financial, commercial and government institutions. These, with the great number of small wholesale and retail traders, formed the nucleus of a growing urban middle class (Campbell and Sherrard, 1968). By the same token the number of workers and marginal men drawn to the capital, increased proportionally.

The face of the city began to change as farmers or impoverished craftsmen from the mountainous villages settled in the periphery of the town, constructing their traditional modest houses and forming distinct neighbourhoods. In their new environment, this population of rural migrants preserved the bonds with their native village, remaining in the same neighbourhood for several generations and keeping their localism and the old mores and customs (Moskof, 1974). Organized as a local association under the leadership of a lawyer or a successful entrepreneur, the communities of compatriots sought to recreate in the city the supporting ingroup network they had known in their native village. The rural migrants who were able to secure permanent employment and were more comfortably off would rent a room or two to the newcomers or to those unable to secure their own shelter.

With the range of industrial production restricted to small shipbuilding and the processing of olives and simple consumer goods, such as textiles and pottery (Campbell and Sherrard, 1968), the number of workers employed in industry was quite limited. Construction of houses and public works, loading and unloading of ships and small-scale transport of goods constituted the occasional employment of the largest number of workers (Moskof, 1974). Manual workers survived mostly through local community support and the subsidies sent from their home villages. The unskilled labourers, constituting the vast majority of the urban working class, were mostly a population of unemployed workers who had to rely for their survival, during the winter months in particular, on the bread, oil and legumes sent by the relatives back in the village (Moskof, 1974). Yet, despite the strong economic dependence of the urban working class on the village community, a paradoxical dissociation is noted in the social sphere between the farmer and the urban worker. As Filias (1974, p. 138) notes, 'the urban dweller, although adhering to a large extent to the rural values and mentality, looks down on the farmer.'

According to Filias and Moskof, this 'paradoxical' dissociation of the Athenian worker from his own roots is a reflection of the attitudes and way of life of the ruling and middle classes, which the migrants emulate in their effort to rise socially and economically. This dissociation of the worker from the peasant way of life is manifested by an aversion for manual work, an idealization of middle class mannerisms, despite their shallowness and superficiality, and the aspiration to an independent job which is nothing more than an unproductive mercenary or parasitic role of a go-between and the 'fetishism of power' (Filias, 1974).

The expectations for economic improvement held by the urban working class led these people to adopt the ruling class values of unproductive consumerism. The corruption and favouritism of the politicians and government officials was a well-acknowledged fact in all of Greece. The continuous pairing of success with favours and privileges accorded by those in power tended to corrode the belief in individual effort, substituting cunningness as a value. As Campbell and Sherrard (1968, p. 275) said, 'The values of Greek society and its institutions do not encourage responsibility either in its people or its politicians.' This disappointing reality, contrasted with the rural ideals for progress through loyalty and hard work, contributed to a growing feeling of malaise for the state of affairs in Greece; a malaise which the working class could not express or translate into action. The only hope the working class Athenian of the time could realistically nourish was for his own personal (i.e. family) advancement, despite and irrespectively of the general state of affairs; an advancement which could only materialize through some fortunate turn of events that would place him next to an influential person offering privileges. In modern Greek parlance, successful people were and still are referred to as the ones that 'grabbed the good . . . opportunity' (*epiase tin kali*). Consistent with this attitude is the working class families' reluctance to give their offspring higher education as opposed to rural families (Dimaki, 1974, p. 132).

On the national level, the repeatedly frustrated hopes for national progress were gradually pinned on the Utopian vision of the Great Idea (i.e. the ambition to redeem the Greeks of the Ottoman Empire and to re-establish the Byzantine *imperium* in the form of a modern Greek state). As was the case with the War of Independence 100 years earlier, every sector of society was aspiring to different gains from this national crusade. In 1921 the crusade was undertaken, resulting in a national disaster with deep repercussions in every aspect of Greek existence.

C. 1922–1940

The settlement of 1 200 000 refugees, who had come to Greece before and during the occupation of Anatolia, was clearly the most serious problem the Greek state had to face. It was a 'moral and practical problem, the solution of which was clearly beyond the unaided resources of the Greek state, bankrupt after the years of intermittent war and political crisis and now called upon to accept a destitute population equal to about one quarter of its own' (Campbell and Sherrard, 1968, p. 138).

The very gravity of the situation and its possible political consequences brought assistance from the international community, both in terms of loans from voluntary organizations and in the establishment of a Refugee Settlement Commission supported by the League of Nations. About half of the refugees settled in the urban centres of Athens and Thessaloniki, since they had not been farmers. Considerable numbers had been artisans, traders and labourers. Professional men, doctors, lawyers and teachers, were also quite numerous (Campbell and Sherrard, 1968). For the urban refugees both housing and working conditions were deplorable. In Athens, overcrowded before their arrival, refugee families lived in barracks and shanties. Although 125 settlements were built by the Commission, 30 000 families were still living under marginal conditions when the Second World War broke out.

With the exception of a limited number of refugees who were officially exchanged in 1922 and were able to bring with them money and valuable goods, the majority of urban refugees became a reservoir of cheap labour. In fact, the second phase of industrial development in Greece was closely related to the refugee problem. The arrival of the refugees gave an impetus to industry in more ways than one. The well-to-do refugees opened workshops and small factories, in some cases introducing skills and manufactures new to Greece; for example, silkworm breeding and carpet-making. Several refugee loans were invested in small Greek industries and the urban population increase provided cheap labour and a widening of the very limited domestic market. It is not accidental, as Campbell and Sherrard (1963) noted, that many factories were built close to urban refugee settlements, where the availability of labour and the pressure of personal needs allowed for a tacit disregard of regulations and agreements on hours of work, wage rates and the employment of women and children.

Although during this second phase of industrial development production multiplied seven times, no departure was noted from the earlier short-term profiteering policy. The basic prerequisites for the foundation of a new industry were a state loan and a tariff privilege that would guarantee a 200–500% increase in the sales price of the imported product, offering the new industry a total control of the local market. Greek industrialists could thus easily afford to buy the second-hand machinery discarded by the European factories. Freed of any pressure to improve their plants they could comfortably deposit their profits in foreign banks and/or invest them in the more profitable shipping business (Rodakis, 1975).

Given this state of affairs, it is no wonder that Greek trade and finance fared very badly under the world trade depression. In 1930 the number of unemployed was 90 000, rising to 180 000 in 1934. The standards of living went down, the purchase value of the daily wages of an unskilled worker in 1929 being 11% below that of 1924 (Goulielmos, 1977). The dissatisfaction of the urban working class was manifested with repeated strikes and an increase of the power of the Greek Communist party. In 1932 there were in Athens and Thessaloniki 200 strikes involving 80 000 workers; 12 000 persons were arrested and 2203 were sentenced to prison (Tsoukalas, 1969).

Despite the political and economic changes brought about by the refugees, both in Athens and in Greece as a whole, their establishment in 'new' settlements on the outskirts of the city did not directly affect the existing social organization of the older Athenian neighbourhoods. Viewing the newcomers with suspicion and controlled hostility, the working class Athenians had as little contact as possible with the refugees, whom they call degradingly Tourkosporites (i.e. of Turkish seed). Nevertheless, after 1922, we can for the first time speak of an urban Greek proletariat. Heterogeneous as it was, this class of people did have in common the marginal living conditions and the memories of a better way of life that was and could no longer be. For the refugees their past life in Anatolia was both more affluent and better organized; for the local population, if their rural past did not offer them any material goods to look back on, it did nonetheless offer a higher quality of life, both in terms of social organization and personal dignity.

A total disillusionment and loss of faith in the future of Greece can be said to be the main characteristic of the Greek and more so of the Athenian scene in the period between the two World Wars. As Campbell and Sherrard point out, 'In the new state of modern Greece the notion of the Great Idea had offered a supra-local loyalty which transcended the opposed parochial interests of village communities . . . The disaster (the military defeat in Asia Minor) choked every breath of idealism . . . no one expects anything of value from Greece' (1968, p. 144). It is in the light of this heritage and the outcome of the civil war (1945–49) that we must attempt to understand the present-day chronicle of civic irresponsibility and unfettered self-interest, which characterizes every aspect of social, political and economic life in Athens.

D. The post-war era

At the end of the civil war Greece was literally in ruins (9000 villages and 23% of all buildings had been destroyed). The course of economic development followed the patterns established during the preceding century. Although the national income has increased steadily since 1949 at an annual rate of about 6%, this economic improvement does not correspond to a sound development of the country's productive resources. In fact the main reasons for the post-war doubling of national income are, according to Mouzelis and Attalides (1971), American aid, the growth of tourism and remittances from the increasing number of Greek emigrants.

Three decades after the civil war, the Greek bourgeoisie has shown no sign of losing its pronounced mercantile character. It remains consumption-oriented and persistently shows a marked reluctance to invest its capital in the industrial sector. Additionally, the foreign economic mission, which virtually ran the country after the civil war, not only failed to encourage industrialization, but even fought against it. When in 1949 a steel mill was given to Greece by the Germans as part of the war reparations, Paul Porter, chief of the USA economic mission, imposed his veto. The machinery never left Hamburg and was eventually sold on behalf of the Greek government as scrap (Tsoukalas, 1969). According to the former representative of Greece to the OECD, Professor Nicolaides, 'Industrialization met with unrestrained reaction mainly because of its effects on the foreign trade of the interested foreign powers, but also largely because of the eventual economic self-sufficiency of Greece which ran counter to their political interests' (Tsoukalas, 1969).

With the attitudes of foreign powers running parallel to the practices of the local bourgeoisie, Greek economy progressed with minute steps, dragging along an ever-increasing structure of parasitic activities. With the continued movement from the countryside to the towns, the need for employment beyond the limited opportunities offered in industry led to the development of new services and new professions. Between 1956 and 1961, 220 000 persons came to Athens from the provinces, and of these 66% came from strictly rural ares. In Athens today the majority of its citizens are still not born in the city. Interestingly enough, no significant difference was ever noted in the occupations of the newcomers and of the original city population. In marked contrast to the inter-war problem of assimilating the Asia Minor immigrants, the new internal migrants are more or less automatically merged with the urban working class (Tsoukalas, 1969).

Usually upon their arrival in Athens the rural migrants settle in the periphery of the city, near or temporarily within the house of a relative or a compatriot through whose guidance they join the ranks of the innumerable persons who manage to make a more or less parasitic living on the fringes of the productive system. 'Small commerce, handicrafts, personal services of all kinds and various intermediary activities (often connected with a para-administrative complex through which the citizen could approach a lethargic and incompetent civil service) involved (in the sixties, and still today) hundreds of thousands of people' (Tsoukalas, 1969).

Although half the country's industry is in the city and 30% of its actively employed inhabitants work in the manufacturing industry, Athens is not an industrial complex. Many workers included in this category are in fact concerned with the repair or assembly of goods rather than their production. The products of Athenian industry are generally light consumer goods (Campbell and Sherrard, 1968). With industry being at an embryonic stage of development, and state finance lacking in credibility, the rising middle classes sought in housing a safe way of investing their profits. Economic considerations, coupled with the traditional dowry system and the floor ownership law passed in 1929, converged to transform an Athens apartment into a most desirable and marketable commodity. This practice took endemic proportions in the seventies, and transformed the face of the city beyond recognition within ten years.

By the late sixties the original refugee suburban communities surrounding the city of Athens had expanded in an unplanned, haphazard fashion; the whole urban complex had spread in all directions as far as the lower slopes of the mountains surrounding the plain. The physical impression of these changes on the outskirts of the city is generally unpleasant; the new settlements in the periphery consist of square, flat-roofed houses, cubes of brick and concrete with one or two rooms only. Very often they stand desolate in a small bare plot of red-brown earth, unfinished for lack of funds, but occupied nevertheless (Campbell and Sherrard, 1968). The narrow strips of earth in front of the houses bear some remote resemblance to a street as they wind across ditches and piles of rubble.

In the older districts of the city the man-made environment has a more urban character. The streets are paved and the old two-storey houses are being replaced by five to seven-storey blocks of flats. In most of these neighbourhoods, which grew without any master plan, the public open spaces are minimal and the roads are extremely narrow. As the apartment block replaces the old house with the yard, the old Athenian residential districts are turned into modern slum areas. Sun, air and the view of a single tree are becoming a rare luxury for most apartment dwellers. The heavy traffic in the narrow streets brings the level of air and noise pollution to alarmingly high levels. Despite the low quality of housing, the cost of these submarginal apartments is quite high.

Housing and land speculation have, for over fifty years, been the most popular form of investment for the middle and lower middle classes. As a result, in all of Greece, and in Athens in particular, the cost of land has increased disproportionately to all other commodities. Since 1975 the price of the smallest flat has become prohibitive for the working classes. Most of the new apartments are in the hands of the middle classes. Young working class couples start their married life in a rented one- or two-room apartment on a one-year lease; living from year to year with the insecurity of a rent increase and the whims of a landlord. In search of a low-rent flat, the young couples today choose their home disregarding all considerations which used to be of prime importance, like proximity to the rest of the family and the ingroup. Thus they find themselves submerged in the anonymity and heterogeneity of the big city.

Tragically enough, the more the quality of life declines the more money is needed in order to secure the basic amenities. In Athens, for example, the traditional gathering of the family and ingroup in the yard is now being displaced to the tavernas and restaurants at a higher cost. Sidewalk cafes attract the people who have no private outdoor space to live in during the summer evenings; and the Sunday ride to a seashore restaurant offers the Athenian families some of the social exchanges which the village square used to provide. In these circumstances, say Campbell and Sherrard (1968, p. 367), 'a family head has the duty to increase his income by almost any means that are not plainly criminal or dishonourable. The social position of his family, which is his sacred trust, requires it. Commercial and personal exploitation, therefore, is often ruthless and, since it is generally suffered by a person outside the social circle of the exploiter, the latter is restrained only by his conscience to which his actions are conveniently justified by a reference to his familial duties. These attitudes have widespread effects in economic (and social) life . . . 'reinforcing the general distrust of men towards one another which is in part a legacy of the opposition and exclusiveness of families in village communities. The difference is that opposition and competition in small traditional communities are contained within a consensus of values sanctioned by public opinion, and are limited by a prudent avoidance of extreme behaviour. In the city there is little to check an individualism the interests of which are wealth, status and consumption.'

Summarizing the basic characteristics of the Athenian working class, it may be stated that it is a marginal population living for the most part in the periphery of the city. It is exposed to all the negative consequences of an urban technological society, but has limited access to all its benefits. It is a population in transition, fluctuating between its rural heritage and the urban reality. Rural by origin, it tries to rise socially above its rural ancestors, adopting an urban way of life and emulating, to the extent possible, the life style of the nouveaux riches middle classes and their opportunistic orienta- tion. In view of the government's total ineffectiveness in securing the basic life amenities, like education, housing, public health and transportation, the Athenian working class clings to the family and ingroup for security, substituting the traditional concept of interdependence for an urban version of it which in operational terms may be translated into: 'I help you and you help me and together we cheat the state or whoever we can.' The continuous effort to make ends meet in the midst of social, economic, political and psychological insecurity drains all their resources and orients their life style to a day to day coping rather than any long-term planning. They have no class or collective consciousness and no loyalty other than to family and friends. Their emphasis is on material acquisitions; yet they nourish a deep longing expressed through popular songs for a simple and harmonious life which is now unattainable, but the memories of which are still vivid.

A people attached, for over 1000 years, to the ideals of honour, loyalty and generosity appears to be turning to opportunism, faithlessness and greed. In October 1981 Greeks opted, on the political level, for change (*alagi*), but what kind of change is really in store for us, on the social and interpersonal level, is hard to tell.

References

Avdelidis, A. (1974). Georgia messa stin economia. *Economicos Tachydromos*, 24 January, Athens.

Brackbill, Y., Adams, G., Crowell, D. H. and Gray, M. L. (1966). Arousal level in newborns and preschool children under continuous auditory stimulation. *Journal of Experimental Child Psychology* **3**, 178–188.

Campbell, J. K. (1964). *Honour, family and patronage*. Clarendon Press, Oxford.

Campbell, J. C. and Sherrard, P. (1968). *Modern Greece*. Benn, London.

Clarke-Stewart, A. (1973). Interactions between mothers and their young children: Characteristics and consequences. *Monographs of the Society for Research in Child Development* **153**, vol. 38, nos. 6–7.

Clogg, R. (Ed.) (1973). *The struggle for Greek independence*. Macmillan Press, London.

Dakin, D. (1973). The formation of the Greek state. *In* R. Clogg (Ed.) *The struggle for Greek independence*. Macmillan, London.

Dimaki, J. (1974). *Pros mian Hellenikin kinoniologian tis pedias*. Social Sciences Centre, Athens.

Du Boulay, J. (1974). *Portrait of a Greek mountain village*. Clarendon Press, Oxford.

Filias, V. (1974). *Kinonia kai exoussia stin Ellada*. Synchrona Kimena, Athens.

Fotiadis, E. (1958). Economiki zoi ton Hellinon kata tin Tourkokratia. *Economiki kai logistiki Encyclopedia* **4**, Athens.

Friedl, E. (1962). *Vassilica, a village in modern Greece*. Holt, Rinehart and Winston, New York.

Goulielmos, P. (1977). *Neohelleniki pragmatikotita* 5th edn. Nea Aristera, Athens.

Huxtable, A. L. (1981). Is Modern Architecture Dead? *New York Review of Books*, 16 July.

Kordatos, G. (1964). *Selides apo tin historia tou agrotikou kinimatos stin Hellada*. 20th Century, Athens.

Lasch, C. (1978). *The Culture of Narcissism*. W. W. Norton and Co. Inc., New York.

Lee, D. (1966). Rural Greece, unpublished notes. Institute of Child Health, Children's Hospital Agia Sophia, Athens.

Meynaud, J. (1965). *Les forces politiques en Grèce*. Lausanne.

Miller, H. (1958). *The Colossus of Maroussi*. New Directions, New York.

Moskof, C. (1974). *Ethniki kai kinoniki synidissi stin Hellada, 1830–1909*. Athens.

Mouzelis, N. and Attalides, M. (1971). Greece. *In* M. S. Archer and S. Ginez (Eds), *Contemporary Europe: class, status and power*. Weidenfeld and Nicolson, London.

Pantazopoulos, N. (1967). *O Kinonikos vios tis Thessalias kata tin Tourkokratian*. Thessaloniki.

Peristiany, J. (1968). *Contributions to Mediterranean sociology. Mediterranean rural communities and social change.* Acts of the Mediterranean Sociological Conference, Athens, July 1963. Paris et la Haye, Mouton.

Rodakis, P. (1975). *Taxis kai stromata stin Neohelliniki kinonia*. Mykinae, Athens.

Runciman, S. (1952). *Byzantine civilization*. Cambridge University Press.

Stoianovich, T. (1953). Land tenure and related sectors of the Balkan economy, 1600–1800. *Journal of Economic History* **XIII**, 402.

Svoronos, N. (1976). *Episkopissi tis Neohellenikis historias*. Themelio, Athens.

Tsoukalas, C. (1969). *The Greek tragedy*. Penguin, Great Britain.

Tsoukalas, C. (1977). *Exartissi kai anaparagogi: o kinonikos rolos ton ekpedeftikon michanismon stin Hellada (1830–1922)*. Themelio, Athens.

Vakalopoulos, A. (1961–74). *Historia tou neou Hellenismou*. A-D, Thessaloniki.

Vassiliou, G. (1966). *Dierevnissi metavliton isserchomenon es tin psychodynamikin tis Hellenikis ikogenias.* Athenian Institute of Anthropos, Technical Report V.

Vassiliou, G. and Vassiliou, V. (1982). Promoting Psychosocial Functioning and Preventing Malfunctioning. *Paediatrician* **11**, 90–98.

Vergopoulos, K. (1975). *To agrotico zitima stin Hellada* 2nd edn. Exandas, Athens.

Weber, A. F. (1968). *The growth of cities in the 19th century*. New York.

Zatz, E. F. (1980). The implications of housing for kinship relations in Exarchia. Paper presented at the 1980 Symposium of the Modern Greek Studies Association, Philadelphia, Pennsylvania.

Index